HEART

KNOWS

ITS OWN

SORROW

By
CAROL E. JAMES

ANSUN
ENTERPRISES
Maryland

ANSUN ENTERPRISES
P.O. Box 1283
Cockeysville, MD 21030

Library of Congress Catalog Card Number: 99-94571

ISBN: 0-9672396-0-5

This book is dedicated to my children

Karen and Kamal

I embrace and love you both

CONTENTS

PAGE

I WANT TO COME BACK AS A TREE

A tree demands and expects nothing
It sees and hears all but does not utter a word
Its stately branches reaches out to the sky
but to no man
It appreciates the cool breeze and elements from the divine
It caresses the elements and shows its appreciation
with new growth and flowing liquids
It provides shelter and protection
for the creatures who must contend with survival
Oh majestic tree towering over all
seeing and knowing all but utters no words

Carol E. James

FAMILY

The thread that binds

HARLEM

In the haze of her restless slumber she could feel faint cramping pains in her abdomen. Subconsciously, she made a mental note that she was about to get her period. As she continued to toss and turn and as the cramping intensified, she became annoyed that her period was coming and the cramping was interfering with her much needed sleep. Then, suddenly her eyes shot open and she sat upright in the bed. Now in a conscious state, she realized the horror of her situation. She was four months pregnant and should not be experiencing cramps. Her period should not be coming. Alarmed and in desperation she reached over and shook her husband, who only a half hour earlier fell asleep after working the graveyard shift at the veterans' hospital. She did not want to disturb him but she needed his assistance. She was miscarrying their child and needed to get to the hospital immediately. He did not awaken at first, then gradually awakened as if from a stupor when she shook him more violently, calling his name in a tone of desperation. In tears she told him that she was experiencing menstrual cramps which meant that she was probably about to miscarry. He abruptly sprang out of the bed, then started searching for his pants, while at the same time asking her if she saw any blood. She checked her panties, which were spotted with blood, and began to cry frantically. He took her in his arms and assured her that everything was going to be all right. Gently, he assisted her with getting dressed, then knocked at their neighbor's door, informed her of the problem and asked her to babysit the other children while they went to the doctor. He called the doctor's office and was told to bring her in immediately.

When they got to the doctor's office she was examined, given a prescription, instructed to rest and to stay off of her feet for a week. A miscarriage was successfully avoided until the same thing happened one month later. This time the doctor asked the couple whether they wanted the child. The husband quickly responded "yes" because he was hoping that the child might be a boy. The doctor gave her a stronger prescription, the same instructions, and assured them that she would not experience the problem again. Four months later she gave birth to a healthy baby girl, marking the beginning of my rocky journey through life. A journey filled with a mixture of disappointments, rejections, sadness, joy and love.

Eight years after my birth, in 1958, my mother shared with me the near miscarriage events, and informed me that my father had hoped I was a boy, since they already had two girls, Vanessa and Nicole. I assume she wanted to please him and that's why she agreed to stop me from aborting myself. She accepted the medication prescribed by the doctor, which prevented the abortion, not knowing the fetus was a girl. I could imagine the disappointment they both felt when I was born. Girl number three. The thought of having another girl had not entered their minds, so when it happened, they had to scramble to think of a name. I was named Carol because my mother thought of Christmas Carols, since the season had just passed. I was described as being long with a small face and a bunch of curly hair. My parents were already struggling to raise and support the children they already had. After me was another girl, Rosetta, who did not try to abort herself, and then two boys, Gregory and Kevin, and another girl, Laura. My mother's oldest child, Richie, was from a previous relationship. We were all raised together and the fact that my oldest brother had a different father was never an issue for any of us.

I often wonder why my mother ever bothered to tell me of the near miscarriages. Was it necessary to inform me that they had hoped I was a boy? I think about that often and have concluded that it was insensitive of my mother to tell me. How was I supposed to feel knowing that when I came into this world, I was a disappointment? I am sure that their disappointment was communicated in some ways to me as an infant, either by touch or not enough nurturing. The effects of their reactions to me were internalized, which eventually affected the way I related to myself, relationships, and people in general. Perhaps, as a mere fetus, I knew that I would not be wanted. Maybe the Universe functions in that manner and all of the unborn can glimpse their impending lives and decide whether they want to live as their lives are pre-designed. Perhaps I as an unborn fetus did not want to undergo the impending disillusionment, confusion, and struggle toward self-awareness, growth, and understanding. The struggle and resistance which ensued between my spirit not wanting to be born and the desires of the almighty spirit resulted in the surrender of my spirit to the will of the all powerful, because I was born. Whatever the reasons why I did not want to be born, and despite the rocky beginning of my life, there were many enlightening experiences, especially in my neighborhood, which helped to shape my character and prepared me to be the person that I became.

Growing up on my block, in Harlem, New York, was full of memorable experiences. It was a time of struggle, in all realms of existence. Most of the people living in my immediate neighborhood were either working people, hustlers, or those receiving some form of public assistance. Those who worked had low paying jobs in both the public and private sectors. So we all struggled financially to survive and live as comfortably as possible. Some were more successful at managing to achieve that feat than others. Most of us learned how to cope with the pressures of living in a deteriorating environment and others surrendered to the pressures of such an atmosphere. For those who were defeated, it was evident in their overall demeanor and the ways they treated themselves and loved ones. Physical and mental abuse existed on many levels. It existed between men and women who abused each other out of feelings of frustration and hopelessness. Children were abused by adults out of ignorance, and feelings of frustration and helplessness. Individuals abused themselves out of self-hate and ignorance. And children abused each other because we were abused and/or out of frustration, powerlessness, and jealousy. Physical aggression and self-destructive behavior were the ways many of us dealt with uncomfortable situations, because we knew no other ways to handle the pains of despair. The abusive behavior was our secret and we kept it from the rest of the world. Only those of us who lived on our block knew of our secrets. The neighbors all knew each other and strived to ensure the safety of the children on the block against any external threats and dangers. No matter the time, there were always adults, who lived on the block, keeping their eyes on the children while we played. Everyone knew exactly where each other lived and could summons help at the first sign of unusual happenings. We knew whenever a stranger lingered on the block and eyes would be watching until that person left. Despite some of our destructive behaviors, we shared loving times, which have created bonds that will last all of our lives.

We lived on 7th avenue between 118th and 119th streets. There were six, five-story identically erected, plain looking brick buildings on the block. The buildings differed only in color. The first two, nearest 118th street, were dark brown with tan window sills, the middle two were brick red with black window sills, and the last two were cream with cream colored window sills. My family lived on the third floor of the first red brick building located in the middle of the block.

Each building had a three feet wide stoop which was used as a hangout for many of the residents, young and old. In the summertime the stoops were occupied at night and during the day by residents trying to escape the overwhelming heat of our apartments. Next to each stoop was a locked metal covering which lead to the basement. During the winter months the metal coverings were opened only long enough for the delivery of coal, which was used to heat the buildings.

Each building had two apartments on each floor. The apartments were described as railroad apartments because of their layout. The rooms were lined up in a straight line so that in order to get from one end of the apartment to the other, we had to go through every room, with the exception of the bathroom. The one and only bathroom was located off the long hall which connected the kitchen to the living room. Needless to say, privacy was almost nonexistent. Given the layout of our apartment and the lack of privacy, I can't imagine how my parents managed to find the time and privacy to have all us children. Amazingly, we never saw them having sex and if we did, we probably did not know what they were doing.

The ground floors of each building housed various businesses, most of which were owned and operated by Black proprietors. The drug store, which was located on the corner of 118th street was owned by a very handsome Black pharmacist who was admired by most of the ladies on the block. He was very low keyed and did not seem to mess around with any of the ladies on the block. If he did have romances with any of them, they were handled very discretely. There were two beauty shops. One was located next to the drug store. Many of the customers that frequented that beauty shop did not live on the block. The proprietor was a loud, boisterous Black woman who had a reputation for being a gossip. The other beauty shop, which was patronized by the women on the block, was located in the building where I lived. Whenever Ma could afford it, she went to that beauty shop. The proprietor was a quiet sweet Black lady who always had a pleasant smile. She dated the super in the building, who was a bum. I often wondered why she dated such a man when, in my opinion, she could do a lot better. There was one candy store that was owned by a dwarf-like, awkward looking Black man who made passes at the young girls. It was rumored that some of the girls would allow him to fondle them for candy and money. That was not unbelievable since many of the children could not afford to buy candy. It was unfortunate that such a predator was amongst us and was able to prey on the ignorant, needy girls in the neighborhood without being detected by the adults. Although the adults on the block were vigilant about making sure that strangers did not violate the children, they were unsuccessful in preventing those, in their own ranks, from committing the very same acts. The other businesses, on the block, were: a grocery store, a taylor shop and cleaners, a barber shop, a Chinese laundry, a coffee shop, a bar, and a small church.

Unlike many other blocks in Harlem, there were no liquor stores on our block. Instead, there was a bar. The people who frequented the bar, which was located in my building, were mostly hard working men who stopped by after work and on Saturday nights. They were decent men who among other things, went there to watch sports, talk trash and play numbers (the illegal predecessor to lottery numbers). The number collectors, better known as number runners, were held in high regard in the neighborhood. They were hustlers who went to each block in the neighborhood taking bets from their patrons. People would bet on single digit numbers or three digit numbers. Many of the number runners were flashy dressing men who drove big cars and had lots of women. The women were attracted to the money and celebrity status of the number runners. Some of the young girls on the block, when they got older, started going with some to the number runners. Back then you were considered a status symbol to be the girlfriend of a number runner, much like it is today to be the drug pusher's girlfriend. After the numbers were finished for the day, it was interesting to watch the number runners and their girlfriends parade around the block sporting fancy clothing and treating the neighborhood children to candy, ice cream and soda. They would go into the bar and buy rounds of drinks for the customers, most of whom had lost a bunch of money playing numbers that day. Everyone knew that if they fell upon serious hardship, they could approach one of the number runners for loans or temporary monetary assistance.

As on every block, we had our share of characters. There was Miss Blair who was going with a married man for about seven years. She depended on his financial help, which he was able to provide since he had a good job at the post office.

He did not live on the block, but became known because of his relationship with Miss Blair. On occasion he would go to the bar and hang out with the fellas, until he started messing around with Miss Blair's best friend, Carnelle, who lived in my building. All hell broke loose when Miss Blair caught them in Carnelle's bed together. The fight between Miss Blair and Carnelle started in Carnelle's bedroom, straight through her apartment, down the stairs and into the street. Both women were pulling each others hair, scratching, kicking and cursing. That continued until the men in the bar broke it up. Embarrassed, because she was clad in only panties and a bra, Carnelle ran back upstairs. Needless to say, that ended Miss Blair and Carnelle's friendship and the married man chose to stay with Carnelle. They eventually had a child together and moved to another neighborhood in uptown Manhattan.

It seemed Miss Blair was wrought with misfortune. Shortly after that incident, she became ill and seldomly went downstairs. Her only child, Andy, became addicted to heroin, started physically abusing her, and demanded the meager money that she managed to scrap together. Unable to defend herself, she would call the cops but, because of the undying love for her son, never pressed charges against him. That abuse continued until she died, unhappy and alone in her apartment. Her body was not discovered until four days after her death, when my mother noticed a foul odor coming from Miss Blair's apartment and realized that she had not seen her looking out of the window for a few days. Andy wept throughout his mother's funeral, and the neighbors wondered

11

who he would find to tolerate his abusiveness, since his mother was no longer alive to do so.

Miss McMillian was a flamboyant woman who, when we moved onto the block, was at least in her sixties. She wore a lot of makeup, long polished nails, low cut dresses and colorful shoes. She lived in the apartment above ours and in the middle of the night, we could often hear the door to her apartment close and shortly afterwards, footsteps and thumps on the floor followed by moaning and groaning. I remember getting up one night, going into Ma's room and asking her about the noise coming from Miss McMillian's apartment. Ma assured me that everything was all right and I should try to ignore the sounds. Once Ma assured me that everything was all right, I never addressed that issue again, although I was often tempted to inform Miss McMillian of how she often disturbed my sleep. Aside from being very active at night, Miss McMillian was also very civic minded. She spearheaded a number of community enhancement projects for which she tirelessly solicited the involvement of the residents from our block and the surrounding area. Most of her projects were successful until people started moving out of the neighborhood and new, less connected people moved in. It was then that the block became littered with garbage because the new residents did not feel the same type of connection that the longer term residents felt. That coupled with the decrease in the Department of Sanitation's services caused the deterioration of our block.

Another interesting person who lived in one of the top floor apartments, in my building, was Mrs. Kate. She was married to a man who worked in a shoe store, owned by a white woman, on the other side of town. They had five children, who were allowed to be in the street all hours of the night. Mrs. Kate often came to our house to speak with Ma. Ma was a compassionate person who always tried to help others. It seemed Mrs. Kate's husband was romantically involved with his white female employer. Often, he did not go home. Moreover, he did not consistently provide financial support for his family. They often had no food or appropriate clothes to wear to school. So, Ma would share some of her food with Mrs. Kate and her children. Ma never told us about Mrs. Kate's problems, but Rosetta and I would sneak and listen to their conversations and hear Mrs. Kate's sobs as she poured out her feelings to Ma. We never let them or Mrs. Kate's children know that we knew what was going on. Even when her children instigated fights against us, we never let them know that we knew their problems. In fact, having knowledge of their problems helped Rosetta and I learn compassion and intensified our love for them. We realized how deeply we cared about them as we all got older and grew closer spiritually. Mrs. Kate was a very friendly, warm hearted woman who always had kind words for us children. However, she always seemed sad, despite her obvious attempts to hide it. As her husband's behavior continued, she eventually started drinking with some of the bums on the block. They would often be seen behind the steps, on the ground floor of the building, drunk and knocked out. That continued until her children became teenagers and started working to assist with the household finances. By that time, their father had moved out of the house and seldomly visited them. They usually saw him at church, where he served as a deacon. The obvious contradictions in his life style made me think about his lack of sincerity to his family and religion. Although I was taught not to pass judgement on other people, it was confusing for me, as a child, to understand what he was doing in regards to sleeping with a white woman, not taking care of his children, professing to be religious, and being very active in the church. In his role as a deacon, he was supposed to be a role model and spiritual advisor to the other parishioners. As I continued to develop as a person, I realized that life was full of contradictions and that situation was just one of them.

To us, everything in our neighborhood seemed to be very normal. We did not realize that our experiences were different from other people who lived elsewhere. The shows that we watched on television "Leave it to Beaver," "Ossie and Harriet," and "Father Knows Best," were perceived as unrealistic, because they depicted suburban, middle class lifestyles that were so different from ours. We had no idea that people actually lived the way those shows depicted life. So that our experiences, like going downstairs to play, were our realities. We played a variety of fun filled games that delighted us from sun up to sun down. My favorite game was Red Rover. It entailed the participants forming two rows about twelve feet apart and facing each other. Each row comprised boys and girls. I always wanted to be on the side of the boy I liked, Pete. He did not know that I liked him, because I did not know how to make him aware of my feelings toward him. So, I settled for holding his hand during the game. As we got older, I felt that he liked me also, but did not know how to tell me. I believe he felt unworthy of me since most people on the block perceived my family as arrogant, proud and untouchable. I yearned for him to approach me and would have felt honored to be in his company. Unfortunately, I did not have the nerve to tell him those things, so we never communicated our feelings to each other.

To play Red Rover, the members of each row would take turns calling a name of a person from the other side to try to bust through any of the outstretched hands held arms of members of the opposing side. We called each other over by saying " Red Rover-Red Rover send _____ right over." If that person failed to bust through the barrier, then he or she would join the other side. That game was quite physical and required the participants to be somewhat strong. Most of the girls did not like playing that game, because the boys would hurt their arms when busting through. I prided myself in being able to withstand the pain and preventing most participants from busting through our barrier. Pete seemed to appreciate that attribute of mine, because we always remained partners.

Other games that we played were: Red light-Green light, the Devil with a Pitch fork, kick the Can, Straight Rope, Double Dutch, Potsy, Lodies, Jacks and many other delightful games. From sun up to sun down there were sounds of children's laughter, but occasionally there were fights. My family was usually involved in the fights because we were the only West Indian family on the block and were mistakenly perceived, by some, as haughty. We did carry ourselves with a certain sense of pride and dignity that was misunderstood as arrogance. My father was born and raised on the Island of Barbuda in the British West Indies. It is one of the Leeward Islands in the Caribbean. During the slave trade, many of the biggest and strongest Africans were brought to Barbuda for breeding purposes. My father said that African Kings and Queens were selected, captured and taken to Barbuda for breeding. He told us to always walk with our heads held high, because we are descendants of royalty. This is probably true because I have noticed that most Barbudans, that I know, are tall, full bodied, good looking and proud. My mother was born in New York but her parents were both from the West Indies. Her father was from Barbuda and her mother, Antigua. They are considered sister Islands. Most of the fights that occurred between my family and other neighborhood children were instigated, for the most part, by Mrs. Kate's children who capitalized on the sentiments of individuals who disliked West Indians. They felt that as West Indians we thought we were better than everyone else. Obviously, they mistook the proud manner in which we carried ourselves, for us thinking that we were better than them. Instead, it was their insecurities that made them feel that way. Rosetta and I thought Mrs. Kates' children were jealous of us and wanted to see us hurt because they did not have much of anything. They wanted us to feel frustration and discomfort, the way they felt each day of their lives. All of us in the neighborhood had similar struggles, like being economically disadvantaged, oppressed and miseducated. Due to our ignorance, we focused on our differences like being West Indian versus Southern, having long hair versus short hair, and being light skinned versus dark skinned. Although asinine, I guess we needed to find reasons to feel superior to each other, since there was little else we had to make us feel good. Unfortunately, we used characteristics that most resembled our oppressors to measure our superiority to each other. Our ignorance and brainwashing caused us to perceive beauty and superiority as what most resembled white people. Therefore, the light skinned individuals were considered more beautiful and desirable than dark skinned individuals. Long, straight hair was more desirable than short, kinky hair. We could not conceive that Black people, regardless of our skin tones, could be legitimate and acceptable. Unfortunately, not much has changed today regarding how we, as Black people perceive beauty, despite the attempts of the 1960's to proclaim "Black is Beautiful." When we looked around our neighborhood, we saw helplessness and hopelessness. The deteriorating buildings, garbage in the streets, and bums on the block, were evidence of extreme despair. The bums were always there and had their places in our lives. We all knew their names and their stories. They were a part of the neighborhood. I guess they reminded us that things could always get worse.

Renny was the oldest and the most responsible of the bums on the block. He worked as the super in our building, if you could call what he did work. Most of the time he was drunk and neglected his responsibilities, so we often went

17

without heat and hot water. The hallways were dirty, especially in the winter when it snowed. Renny would not mop the floors for months, regardless of how much the residents complained to management. However, Renny was not always a bum. He grew up in a rural area in South Carolina, and at the age of seventeen took a bus to New York City, where he found work as a cleaning boy in a grocery store. He was hard working and had plans of finishing school and joining the army. Unable to get enrolled in school, he joined the army and fought in the Korean War. While there, he sustained a head injury and underwent extensive surgery. Since that operation Renny had not been right in the head, including experiencing bouts of forgetfulness. He married shortly after being discharged from the army to a woman ten years older and they had five children. During his marriage, unable to hold a steady job, he began drinking. As his drinking progressed, his wife insisted that he leave. With no place to go, he ended up taking a super's job in our building. Renny was always very polite and treated the children nicely. Although he drank a lot, he never became boisterous or disrespectful.

On the other hand, Blue was a very loud and boisterous bum who, when drunk, was totally obnoxious, fresh and despicable. No one on the block liked him. He was shunned and on occasion, run off the block by various individuals fed up with his antics. He would leave for a few days but always managed to return begging the proprietors for work. They allowed him to sweep and mop their facilities for a meager wage. He slept in the back of the various hallways on the block. No one seemed to know much about his background except that he served some time in jail. I never trusted him and felt he was capable of becoming inappropriate with the children. On several occasions he said things to me that I did not understand, but I felt, from his demeanor were inappropriate. Rosetta and I shared the same feelings about him and vowed if he ever touched us, we would beat him up.

Mousy was the other disgusting bum on our block. He would get sloppy drunk and use loud, foul language, laying slovenly wherever he happened to be when the booze got to his head. He had a big disgusting pot belly that always seemed to be exposed and had extremely big hanging pink lips that always dribbled. Of all of the bums on the block, he was the most disgusting. It seemed everybody disliked him and because of his nasty, disrespectful manner, he was always getting beat-up and left bleeding in the street. He was so disliked that bums from other blocks would come on our block to beat him up. He was a thief, a beggar and a liar. Some people said he came from a good home down South, but found his wife in the bed with another woman, and he'd been drinking since then.

It seemed we all shared a sense of anger and frustration, and because we did not know how to manage our feelings, would always beat-up on each other, just like the bums did to Mousy. Those fist fights played an important role in my life. They were a way for me to release frustration and exercise some semblance of power, since the environment rendered me powerless. Most of the fights, that I engaged in on a daily basis, stemmed from other children calling me names. I was brown skinned, with long hair, tall and slim. Most of the children thought I was skinny, especially the boys. I preferred to refer to my physical stature as slim. The names, that the children called me, were demeaning and hurtful: Long John Silver, Jolly Green Giant and Olive Oyle. Therefore, I disliked pirates, canned vegetables and the Popeye cartoon. Whenever the children taunted me, I would lash out and demonstrate my powerful wrath regardless of whom they were; boys, girls, younger, older, big or small, it did not matter. Well, there was one exception. A girl who lived around the corner from my house, named Geraldine. I was petrified of Geraldine. Whenever she came on the block, no matter what I was doing, I stopped and ran upstairs. Geraldine was a big burly bully who looked like a boy. She was heavy set and could fight. I knew I was no match for Geraldine, so I ran whenever I saw her. Looking back at the situation, Geraldine probably wasn't even thinking about me most of the time. In fact, the only time that I can remember her bullying me was one day when I was downstairs playing Double Dutch with my sister Rosetta and some friends. I didn't see Geraldine coming because my back was facing her street. All of a sudden she was there trying to jump into the rope. I dropped the rope and ran upstairs. Gingerly, I looked out of the window, in my mother's room. To my surprise, I saw my younger sister Rosetta hitting Geraldine with her shoe. I was stunned at the sight. Amazingly, Geraldine did not hit her back. I don't know whether it was because she was much bigger than Rosetta and did not want to hurt her or that she admired Rosetta's nerve. Whatever it was, she just left. Well, I did not go downstairs for the rest of the day and Geraldine never caught me off guard again. To this day I wonder whether Geraldine was the horrible person I thought she was or whether it was only my childish imagination.

It seemed I was always fighting although I did not enjoy it, like my sister Rosetta did. She loved to fight. Although not a bully, she found herself defending the weaker children, who were not skillful enough to defend themselves. Whenever the bullies picked on children who Rosetta liked, she would step in and defend them with a vengeance. When she fought, it seemed to transform her into another dimension of time and space, oblivious to feeling pain or realizing the amount of pain she was inflicting on others. The magnitude of her anger was astounding. I on the other hand, although proficient in defending myself, did not possess the skill, delight or intensity as Rosetta. Living in that environment in some respects was similar to the way animals have to survive in the wilderness. Utilizing the concept of survival of the fittest, Rosetta was clearly a survivor. That type of environment was a microcosm of the world in general. For example, wars waged on weaker, vulnerable countries by the more powerful, mightier nations who trample the weaker countries and rob the inhabitants of their dignity, property and natural resources. However, the more dominant nations find ways to justify their behaviors, but show disdain for people in poor neighborhoods who emulate the same behaviors as they.

Unlike most of the parents on the block, my parents did

not allow us outside at night because more unsavory and dangerous activities occurred at night. So Rosetta and I were content looking out of the window until all hours of the night. The window was located in my parents' room but they did not mind us in their room so late. My father worked nights at the Veterans Hospital and my mother was happy knowing that we were home and away from trouble. We got a real education about the things that happened on the streets of Harlem, by looking out of that window. In fact the window gave us a better vantage point than those individuals hanging out in the streets whose view were limited to their immediate surroundings. For instance, the number runners could not see the cops approaching two blocks away, yet Rosetta and I could see them from the window. We also saw that Carnelle was messing with Miss Blair's married man months before she caught them together. At night, from the window, we saw him sneak into our building and then heard Carnelle's door close each time. Hours later, we would see him leave our building and go into the next building where Miss Blair lived. From the window, we saw that the pimp could not keep track of what his prostitutes were doing on each of six corners, because of his limited range of view. Rosetta and I, however, could see how many tricks they turned and how fast. We saw pimps beating up their prostitutes and prostitutes running down the streets naked, to get away from the angry wrath of their pimps. We even saw some of the girls we grew up with eventually become involved with the pimps, and become prostitutes on the other blocks. I guess they always admired how fine those pimps looked, at night, in their flashy clothes and their charming personalities towards the children. During the daytime, the pimps dressed like regular folk and took time to play ball with the boys and lead the girls in some of our games. They seemed so sweet and loving. But Rosetta and I knew the other side of the pimps that emerged at night, on the other blocks. We saw those pimps beating their prostitutes when the other girls were playing downstairs and could not see what was happening on the other blocks, oblivious to the pimps' other highly volatile side. I was able to observe the way pimps operated, as a child, which enabled me, in later years, to identify and avoid unsavory characters with pimp-like approaches. Growing up in that environment was a learning experience. We observed and learned things that were not taught in school. We learned how to survive in a hostile environment. We learned how to observe and perceive people and determine their motives, we learned how to be insightful.

From the window, we saw when drugs were introduced into the neighborhood. One by one, the older boys on the block got strung out on heroin. For the most part, those who did not get strung out ended up getting drafted and served in Vietnam, where some ended up getting strung out anyway. Some died in Vietnam and those who survived came back with horrible memories of death and destruction. Pete, the guy I had a crush on, was one of those who, unfortunately got strung out on drugs in Vietnam. That seemed most unfortunate because he came from a very dysfunctional family. His mother was an alcoholic and his father was not around.   Pete and his five siblings were raised by an overwhelmed grandmother who seemed to have little control over the children.   With the exception of Pete, as the children reached puberty, they engaged in criminal activities, robbing taxi cabs, snatching pocketbooks, and using drugs. It seemed Pete went into the service to get away from the negative influences in the neighborhood. It was his way of avoiding the drugs and criminal activities, however, he was not prepared for the horrors of Vietnam. To cope, he started smoking dope in Vietnam and brought that habit back to New York with him. After years of being strung out on dope, he was found dead in an abandoned building three blocks away from where we grew up. His was truly a sad situation. He survived the hardships of his childhood, the drugs and crime on the streets of Harlem, only to go away to a far off land, to fight for his country, and end up in the same predicament that he could have been in without leaving home. When he returned from Vietnam and I learned that he was strung out on heroin, I wept for him and wondered if things could have been different if I had the courage to tell him how I felt about him. After his return from Vietnam and whenever Pete and I saw each other, usually each year at our block's reunion during the African Day Parade, he would try to avoid eye contact with me, but I always embraced him with a genuine loving hug as if to try to make up for the cowardice of my earlier years.

From the window, we also saw the times when my oldest brother, Richie, had to run home because gang members tried to beat him up, because he refused to join a gang. Gangs were prevalent in Harlem, back then. It was difficult for a teenage boy to survive in the neighborhood without being a gang member. Richie and his friends had no desire to join gangs. Their families and friendships provided all the sense of belonging they needed. Unlike the surrounding blocks, the boys on our block did not belong to gangs and the adults worked hard to provide them with positive reinforcement against joining gangs. They felt if one boy joined, then most likely others would follow. There were many days Richie had to fight. Many days he came home with bruises and several times Ma had to go to the police precinct to report the assaults and threats against him. Often the police tried to avoid dealing with the situations, but my mother was persistent. She was a strong willed woman who refused to let the street elements consume my brother and the rest of us. Ma did not hesitate to suggest to the policemen, whenever they tried to avoid investigating Richie's problem with the gangs, that they should concentrate on assisting the young decent neighborhood children instead of harassing the number runners who were more helpful than harmful to the community.

Raising eight children all with different strong personalities was not an easy task. Richie was the man of the house, since my father was not actively involved in the household because he was either sleeping, working, or somewhere gambling. It is not unusual, even today, to find that the older siblings in large, economically disadvantaged families, have adult-like responsibilities in the families which is quite unfortunate as it deprives them of their childhood. When my

mother was not at home, Richie was in charge. He assigned
us chores...only he made it fun. We would act like he was
the sergeant and we were the privates and buck privates. Off
we would march to do our assigned chores under the
supervision of the sergeant. I realize now, but did not then,
Richie never had any assigned chores when we played that
game. He was shrewd, bossy and would not hesitate to give
us a whack or two if we disobeyed him. All of us were afraid
of our big brother Richie although he also demonstrated love
for us in his own tough way. He was held with great esteem
by people on the block, as well. He was a natural leader and
handled himself well. Everybody liked Richie and knew that
they could depend on him to run errands, fight their battles
and be a support. As a young child, he would say that he was
going to be a cop when he grew up. Whenever he was
attacked by guys from other blocks, he swore to get them
back when he became a cop.

Richie always liked to play in a rough manner, like picking
you up and turning you upside down, play fighting and
dinging you up side your head. I was not down for that and
made it known, but Rosetta loved it. She often waited for
Richie to come home so they could play fight. Richie said it
made us tough. It worked for Rosetta because she could
really fight, and loved every moment of it. Richie especially
worked on my two younger brothers, Gregory and Kevin,
because they were boys and were expected to be able to
defend themselves and their sisters. Although those were
Richie's expectations of them, quite often, Rosetta had to
defend them against the other children in the neighborhood.

Gregory got the worse of Richie's rough treatment because he had a slight switch when he walked and Richie said that no brother of his was going to be a fagot. By the time Gregory was nine, the switch was gone.

When Richie was in the eleventh grade, he approached Ma and told her that he wanted to quit school to go to work to be of more financial help to the family. He was already working after school, at a neighborhood luncheonette. I remember, he would come home at night with pies or whatever was left over that could not be sold the next day. On pay days he would bring his money home and give it all to my mother. She would give him an allowance and give all of us other children a quarter or fifty cents, depending on our ages. Richie never complained. My mother was outraged at Richie's suggestion of quitting school, and told him that everything was going to be alright. She explained that he was doing enough and could be even more helpful after he received his high school diploma and could get a better job.

For a time that quelled his desire to leave school, but not for long. In a short time, he devised a plan to play hookey and get thrown out of school. That was a major mistake. Evidently, he underestimated Ma. When she learned of his absences from school, she started taking him to school. Richie was quite embarrassed; he was a seventeen year old being taken to school by his mother. His friends laughed at him but only behind his back because they were afraid to let him see them laughing. Richie pleaded with Ma to stop escorting him to school and eventually agreed to attend school each day on his own and graduate. He kept his word, graduated and joined the Army shortly after. It was a solemn day in our household when Richie went into the service. From our windows, we watched him walk towards the subway until he was out of sight. All eyes were filled with tears. Ma tried to be brave for the rest of us, but as his figure began to disappear from sight, a painful, wrenching sob that could only come from a mother was heard.

While in the service, Richie sent his monthly checks home. He reenlisted and served a total of six years, and during that time got married to a long time friend. They had a son, but the marriage did not last. Shortly after getting out of the service, they divorced. Richie became a cop and did have occasions to arrest many of the guys from the neighborhood who used to beat him up. Unfortunately, they became involved in illicit behavior which placed them in the position of having to face the person, now a cop, who they once mistreated. As Richie said, "what goes around, comes around."

My oldest sister, Vanessa, was brown skinned, heavy set with a pretty face. Ma did not seem to like her. Vanessa was born two months premature and was hospitalized for six months before she was well enough to come home. Those six months were very stressful for Ma. Each day she would have to arrange for someone to watch Richie while she went to the hospital to see Vanessa, who had undergone several life threatening operations. So during the six months, Ma and Vanessa did not develop a bond. Ma could not hold Vanessa until she was out of the incubator, which took several months. During that time, she began to view Vanessa as more of a burden than a bundle of joy and that attitude persisted throughout Vanessa's childhood. Ma always seem- ed to be aggravated with Vanessa, who like me, had a reading problem but was not shrewd enough to hide it. So, Ma knew about Vanessa's reading problem and tried to help her, the best way she knew how, but it was the wrong way. Ma would hit Vanessa whenever she forgot words, leaving her a nervous wreck. I was no fool. After seeing that, I decided my secret would be with me forever. It seemed as though Ma would take her frustrations out on Vanessa, many of which had nothing to do with Vanessa. Ma would be frustrated with Daddy not giving her the love, appreciation, support and attention that she desperately needed. So when Vanessa presented her problem which required Ma to give even more of herself without getting the gratification that she needed from Daddy, she took her feeling of frustration out on Vanessa. My father always complained about the way Ma treated Vanessa and often came to her rescue whenever he saw Ma mistreating her. However, Vanessa would take advantage of my father's compassion for her and use it as an opportunity to ask him for things she wanted. She had a knack for catching him at his most vulnerable times to solicit anything from candy to clothes to money from him. He relented because she was unrelenting with her sobbing and begging.

The deprivation that she experienced as an infant, not having the opportunity to receive her mother's loving caresses, was the precipitating factor to Vanessa's poor relationships with people. She, like Rosetta, was a fighter and did not hesitate to fight the worse children in the neighborhood. She made Geraldine, the girl I was deathly afraid of, look like a girl scout. When Vanessa was around, no one called me names. Even the older boys did not mess with Vanessa. She was in what was called "opportunity classes" which is the same thing as today's "Special Education Classes." Many of the children in those classes were emotionally challenged and Vanessa was one of the leaders in the class. She feared nothing and tended to hang out with the worst children in the school. I guess Vanessa had so much rage in her, she had to release it somehow, so she did it by fighting. Not only did she fight at school and in the neighborhood, she also fought at home with me. Our relationship was antagonistic. We did not get along with each other and I often felt her wrath. She was a liar, sneaky and selfish. All of the qualities I disliked in a person. I would often catch her hiding in bed hoarding candy, so she wouldn't have to share with the rest of us, and then would leave the wrappers behind the bed. She and my brother Gregory were also responsible for all of us getting beatings, because they would drink most of the juice and soda out of the containers. Then they would fill the containers up with water and place them back in the refrigerator. When Ma asked who did the acts, they would not confess, so we all had to get beatings. After the beatings, I would call Vanessa derogatory names related to her unscrupulous behavior and she would then retaliate by whipping my ass. I tried to put up a fight, but was no match for her. However, I got satisfaction in letting her know that I knew what she was doing and how I felt about it. Although Vanessa and I did not get along, she did get along with Richie. I guess he liked her fighting spirit. She was in competition with Nicole for my mother's attention and she distanced herself from the younger siblings.

Vanessa hated living at home and often voiced her desire to leave. Her opportunity came when she met a recently arrived Barbudan immigrant. He had only been in this country one month, when they met. They had gone out on a blind date that was arranged by Nicole's boyfriend, Tyson, when Vanessa was seventeen years old. Vanessa never had a real boyfriend before meeting Allen. Although she liked a few of Richie's friends, they knew that Richie prohibited dates between his sisters and his friends. If they tried, it was inevitable that they would be beaten up unmercifully by Richie, so they did not try, although it was obvious that a few of them liked us. After a brief courtship of five months, at the age of eighteen, Vanessa married Allen, who was twenty-six years old. After their marriage, they owned and operated a successful wall paper business and remained disconnected from the rest of the family because of the way Ma showed favoritism among her children.

Nicole was Ma's favorite. She was light skinned with sandy brown hair, heavy set but her face was not as pretty as Vanessa's. Whenever Ma described Nicole, she always referred to her as "pretty, smart and high yella." How could Nicole not feel good about herself if Ma, from the time Nicole was born, praised her and put her on a pedestal. Compared to the treatment Vanessa received, Nicole received the type of positive reinforcement that destined her for success. I often wondered if Ma's feelings for Nicole would have been the same if Nicole had been dark skinned. Unfortunately, Ma was one of those ignorant black folk who defined beauty by the hue of one's skin. Ma always allowed Nicole to sit around reading while Vanessa had to do the dirty chores. Nicole's responsibility was to take care of my youngest sister, Laura, who was the baby of the family. That did not seem like much of a chore at all. She enjoyed combing Laura's hair, dressing her up and taking her out to play. They were always together and Laura thought that Nicole was her mother. It wasn't until she reached puberty that she realized Nicole was not her mother. Even today, Nicole and Laura continue to maintain a close bond.

My relationship with Nicole has always been strained. From the day I was brought home from the hospital, the rivalry began. My parents, not knowing any better, had not properly prepared Nicole for my arrival. Nicole was three years old when I was born. The crib had been her bed since birth, until the day I was brought home from the hospital and placed in the crib. Ma and Daddy had failed to wean her from sleeping in the crib, so when I took over her bed, she was not pleased. That night she proceeded to remove me from the crib, placed me on the floor and got into the crib. That was the beginning of our rivalry. To this day I am convinced that had my parents received the proper knowledge and parenting skills regarding how to prepare children for the impending arrival of a newborn into the family structure, Nicole and I would probably be better friends than we are today. That is why it is important for expectant parents to take advantage of the parenting information available and obtain the knowledge they need to avoid unnecessary and unpleasant family situations.

Unlike the rest of my siblings, I voiced my displeasure with the way Ma favored Nicole over the rest of us. Ma had a habit of asking Nicole for advice, because she thought Nicole was well read and knew everything. However, I voiced my opposition whenever her responses made no sense to me. I baulked at the idea that Nicole had to be right and everyone else was wrong. In my opinion, we all had a right to our opinions and should be allowed to voice them. Daddy was also disgusted with the way in which Ma blatantly displayed her favoritism towards Nicole, however he did not have the fortitude to constantly confront her. Although Daddy, Vanessa and I had strong feelings about the unfairness of it all, the rest of the children didn't seem to care. The three youngest children Gregory, Kevin and Laura were too young to care about such issues. They were content with being cared for, no matter who performed the tasks. Unfortunately, when it came to the dirty work, Nicole was excluded. So, they tended to call upon Vanessa to handle the unpleasant tasks related to their care. My involvement with them was minimal. I was consumed and satisfied with my inseparable relationship with Rosetta.

MIDDLE CHILDREN

Rosetta and I were the middle children. I was the fourth and Rosetta was the fifth. As a result of being stuck in the middle, we got the least amount of attention from other members of the family, which caused us to depend upon each other for attention and support. We seemed to be the forgotten entity, however, I made sure that I got my recognition from time to time. Our relationship transcended the normal sibling relationship. We were spiritually connected. Often, we could tell what each other was thinking and found ourselves completing each other's sentences. Even today, our children complain that we say the same things, so they do not bother to seek out the other for a differing opinion. They also know that no matter what, we support each others decisions. We have always had an unbreakable bond. Even when we get angry with each other, we speak our minds, go someplace to cool off and then return as though nothing had happened.

As children, we did everything together and enjoyed each

other's company immensely. Rosetta was dark brown skinned, medium height and build, quiet, reserved and took no mess from anyone. I, on the other hand, was loquacious, gregarious and took a lot of mess from people. We complimented each other. We were the exact opposites with the exception of our tastes in clothes. Our taste in clothes were so similar that one Christmas we happened to buy each other the exact same sweaters. We developed our classy taste in clothes by observing some of the people who frequented the bar, some of the number runners and hustlers. As children, looking out of the window, we admired the way many of the bar patrons dressed. Their clothes were always color coordinated, of good quality and stylish. But other than our taste in clothes, we were opposites and it's true, opposites attract, because we were inseparable. Wherever one was, the other one was there also. In fact, whenever we were not together, people always asked about the other one.

Although I got good grades in school, Rosetta was an honor student and attended classes for the intellectually gifted at a predominately white school in the Bronx. She attended that school as a result of bussing legislation, which enabled children to be bussed to schools outside of their immediate neighborhoods. She was at the top of her class and received many awards, which, for the most part, went unrecognized by my parents. Daddy was not around to notice. Ma only recognized Nicole's accomplishments, which did not come close to the level of excellence as Rosetta's. Rosetta never complained although I noticed that she seemed to have a quietly sad demeanor. At home, she never demanded any attention from anyone. It was as though she did not exist. I on the other hand demanded attention. Unfortunately, I did not receive attention automatically either, but unlike Rosetta, I did not accept being disregarded, so I devised a way of getting attention by using my Asthma. As a young child, I realized that whenever I got sick, my parents and grandmother gave me extra special attention. They took me to the hospital, allowed me to sleep in their beds and spoon fed me. So whenever I needed attention, I ate something that would cause me to get an asthma attack. Rosetta, however, did not devise such antics. She just accepted being unnoticed.

Rosetta's overall demeanor has always been pleasing, although she seldom smiled. As a child, she distanced herself from most of the drama that occurred between her siblings. Quiet and observant, she accepted life the way it was and thrived academically. I really liked Rosetta and always admired her cool, quiet sense. Her biggest fault was that she could not sing, although she often tried. Her singing was so bad that one day, while we were fooling around in the living room, she started singing. She sounded horrible, so horrible that I started feeling sick and pleaded with her to stop. She thought I was joking and continued to sing. Well, that ended up to be one of the worse Asthma attacks I ever had. Ma had to call an ambulance and I was taken to Harlem Hospital for treatment. To this day she knows what to do to keep me in line. All she has to do is threaten to sing and I will be cool. As we got older and she went along with me through some of my outlandish escapades, her steadfastness and common sense has always been reassuring for me. We were always together. One of my male friends, a very shady character, always referred to Rosetta as "riding shotgun" which means, always watchful, alert and ready to protect and act as necessary. He always kept an eye on her, and she did the same with him. If he had ulterior motives, he dared not try anything when Rosetta was around.

We were best friends, but at the age of nine I learned there were limits to the types of things I could share with Rosetta. One evening while we were washing and drying the dinner dishes, I decided to share with Rosetta a conversation that took place at school that day regarding one of the neighborhood girls. I was told by one of my classmates that the girl "did pussy" with one of the boys at school. Of course I had no idea what pussy was but acted as though I knew so as not to be perceived as being lame. I told my best friend, good buddy, confidante, Rosetta, about the conversation. To my surprise, she immediately said "Uhhhhh, I'm gonna tell Ma." With that she proceeded to drop the dish cloth and walk towards Ma's room. I was stunned. Was my best friend going to tell Ma on me? I pleaded with her not to tell but she did. Ma came after me with a belt and I ran onto the fire escape trying to elude the beating that was sure to come. By that time I deduced that doing pussy was something bad, whatever it was. From that day on I knew there were some things I could not tell Rosetta. However, that did not jeopardize our loving relationship. We continued to enjoy each other's company and managed to interact with the rest of the family especially during the holidays.

Christmas was always a joyous time for my family. Although my parents did not have much money, in fact we struggled to survive, somehow Ma always made sure that we had presents under the tree. I remember writing to various organizations for donations and standing on long lines to receive toys. I always disliked standing on those lines, in the cold. Although the organizations were doing good deeds by providing toys to the economically disadvantaged, they made us feel like beggars unworthy of being invited inside. Instead, we had to wait on long lines in the cold, only to walk up to a door and be handed a toy. I remember standing on those long lines and vowing that when I had children, I would never put them in the predicament of being so humiliated. Sometimes, people who are emotionally, economically and socially removed from the people they wish to help, wind up causing more pain and discomfort to those same people because of their insensitivity to what they perceive as small matters. If they truly want to be respectful to the people they wish to help, they would spend more time finding out, from them, how best to do so.

Ma always managed to buy some extra toys to go along with the donated ones. Therefore, it always seemed as though we had a lot. She would start purchasing toys after Christmas, for the next Christmas. Then she used a great deal of creativity to hide them from us. Most of the time she asked our cousin Ester, Daddy's niece, who was ten years older than Ma, to store the things in her apartment until Christmas. Cousin Ester and her husband lived on 119th

Street between 7th and Lenox Avenues. They were permanent fixtures in our house whenever we had any sort of celebration. They were there for every holiday, birthday, Christening, party, and always gave us very nice gifts. They did not have any children, so they really appreciated being a part of our festivities. We loved them and did not mind running errands for them, especially since they gave us handsome tips. Both of them were hard working people, who seemed to have more money than they needed. When Ma really needed money, she could always depend on cousin Ester for a loan.

No matter how cold it was on Christmas, Rosetta and I would go downstairs with at least one of our new toys. I remember the year we received Patty Play Pal dolls. They stood approximately two feet tall and were white with long hair. We took them downstairs and played with them for hours, combing their hair and playing house. When we got too cold, we went upstairs, got in the bottom bunk bed, threw the covers down from the top bunk so as to enclose the bottom bunk, and played house. We were so happy because we had our dolls and tea sets. When we got tired of playing house we played hospital with our doctor and nurse bags we received as gifts from a previous Christmas. To play hospital we recruited one or two of our younger siblings to be patients. Although they sometimes wanted to be the doctor or nurse, we would not allow them that privilege. That was reserved for me and Rosetta, since the doctor and nurse bags belonged to us. There weren't many games all of us children played together, but one that we found to be most rewarding was school. Nicole was an avid reader and always wanted to play school. This enabled us to get some extra tutoring, which I desperately needed, since I had a reading problem. Rosetta was a whiz in school, so she was not that impressed with playing school. I, however was able to convince her to play and that way was able to receive special help from her without her knowledge. Nicole always wanted to be a teacher. She was good at playing school and eventually, in real life, became an elementary school principal.

There were hours upon hours of fun. We always managed to have fun no matter what season or circumstances. Rosetta and I were the masters at finding fun things to do. During the summertime, we would go out on the fire escape to play with our neighbors in the next building who were not allowed to go downstairs to play with the other children. In fact, we were the only children with whom they were allowed to play. Ma said, they were allowed to play with us because we were decent and respectful. That always troubled me because I felt the other children on the block were decent and respectful too. Rosetta and I thought they did not play with the other children because they were very light skinned, and their parents thought they were too good to play with the other children. Even though we were brown skinned, they probably felt their children had to play with some kids, so it just as well be the ones who were not allowed to stay in the streets at night.

We had such good times playing on the fire escape. One of our favorite games involved sending notes back and forth via a rope. We made the rope into a pulley, attached a basket and sent the basket back and forth with the notes. Sometimes when it was very hot, we would drape our blankets over the top of the fire escape and play underneath the blankets. We never thought about the dangers of playing on the fire escapes. We were cautious and skilled at it. In the 19 years that we lived on 7th Avenue, only one boy fell off a fire escape. He had been doing acrobatic tricks and miscalculated a jump. He broke a leg and after mending, continued to play on the fire escape.

Dangling our feet through the opening of the fire escape Rosetta and I would watch the older boys play stick ball in the backyard. The backyard was often littered with garbage that residents threw out of their windows, since the dumb waiters were no longer being used because they caused rats to come into the buildings. Of course, throwing garbage into the backyard did not remedy the problem, but people just wanted the garbage out of their apartments as quickly as possible, so without forethought, we threw it in the backyard. Rats were everywhere. At night we had to barricade ourselves in the rooms by putting boxes in front of the broken french door windows in order to keep the rats out of the bedrooms. In the middle of the night, we would hear the sounds of the rats banging their bodies against the boxes trying to get into the bedrooms.

One day there was a big sick rat dying in the kitchen and Daddy and Richie were not home. The rest of us were too afraid to go near it, so we called our next door neighbor, Mr. Sampson who made a gallant effort to fight the rat off with a broom, but the rat won the battle sending Mr. Sampson back home. Our downstairs neighbor Carnelle heard the commotion and came upstairs to find out what was going on. When we explained the situation, Carnelle sucked her teeth, pushed us aside, picked up the broom, proceeded to whip that rat to death, cleaned up the mess and went back downstairs. Rosetta and I stood in amazement. When we recovered, after about 2 minutes, we started laughing and slapping five. Carnelle was B-A-D.

The rat problem in the building was bad, but the roach problem was worse. Although Ma had us work feverishly to keep the house clean, we could not manage the infestation of roaches. We seldom saw roaches in the bedrooms, but they loved hanging out in our kitchen. There were thousands of them all over the cabinets, ceiling and floor. They came out when we turned off the lights. We dreaded needing to go into the kitchen at night, after the lights were turned off. To reenter the kitchen at night, we had to walk, stomping our feet, down the long hall leading to the kitchen. The light string was in the middle of the kitchen, which meant we had to enter the kitchen before being able to turn on the light. Once inside the kitchen and after turning on the light, without fail, at least a few dozen roaches would fall off of the ceiling, some falling on us. We would brush them out of our hair and off of our clothes. Rats and roaches made living in our apartment uncomfortable. It was a never ending battle between us, the rats and roaches, which we saw as the normal course of life in Harlem. We never saw those kinds of things on the television programs we watched. Life was depicted in those programs as wonderful, and free of rats and roaches.

Rosetta and I did find ways of coping with the uncomfortable aspects of our life style. I was the outgoing one who always managed to get us involved in crazy escapades and Rosetta would go along to "watch my back." So we found ourselves starting a club comprised of some of the girls, who we liked, from the block. It started as a result of one little girl by the name of Nisa, who had no siblings. She lived with her grandmother, who worked, and two cousins who intermittently stayed with them. Nisa was lonely and always came by our house to ask us if we could have company or whether we could go downstairs to play. Nisa's mother seldom came around and when she did, she appeared to be intoxicated. Nisa was somewhat of an outcast. The other children on the block did not play with her very much because she was unattractive, by the standards we used to judge attractiveness in those days. In retrospect, I consider her to have been quite attractive. She had smooth very dark brown skin, big protruding eyes, short hair and a very thin build. I remember Rosetta and I were at Nisa's house listening to the Coasters' record *Charlie Brown* and acting out the skit that the group used to do. We knew the skit because we were avid Apollo goers. Then, we got the idea to perfect our skit and have a show for the other kids on the block. Everyone would have to pay five cents admission. As we continued to develop the idea, we thought about how we would promote the show, what costumes would be needed, where we would have it and other details. We realized we needed more people to be involved with the show if it was going to be a success. Hence, Our Club was born.

I used my gifts of persuasion to recruit some of the girls on the block, while Rosetta watched my back and Nisa looked shyly about with pleading eyes. Three other girls joined our club, two sisters and one of my classmates. We worked hard to prepare for the show. Our planning, organizational and promotional skills were pretty good. Everyone was assigned responsibilities and had to report their progress at our meetings. The show took place at the home of the two sisters since no one else could persuade their parents to allow the show to take place in their homes. It was well attended. Most of the boys on the block came because they liked the two sisters and wanted to earn brownie points with them. The show was hilarious and I played *Charlie Brown*, the clown. After the show, the boys ridiculed me every chance they got about my funny looks which were exaggerated for the skit and of course, we fought.

The Club continued for a few more months. We would go to the five cent movie theater at least one Saturday a month. For that five cents we saw the main feature, two cartoons, a news reel and a short, which occupied most of the day. In those days you got a lot for your money. However, there was a drawback to going to the five cent movie theater, perverts. It seems weird men hung out in that movie theater, so before going, we girls worked out a strategy. We all were to stay together no matter what. If one person had to go to the bathroom, then we all had to go together. Our strategy worked until one day a pervert came and sat next to me. I choose to sit on the last seat because I was not afraid. He came and sat next to me even though there were plenty of empty seats elsewhere. I knew then that his intentions were not honorable. So I nudged Rosetta, to put her on alert. We always were able to communicate accurately without saying a word. Rosetta checked out the situation and motioned to me her awareness. Well, shortly after the main feature began, the pervert started making groaning sounds and I noticed that he was moving his hand up and down his crotch. In the heat of excitement, he placed his other hand on my thigh and started caressing it. Why did he go there? That was a big mistake. I stood up and started shouting him out about how sick he was playing with himself and trying to get fresh with me. I yelled to the top of my lungs and Rosetta and I started kicking and beating him up. He did not hang around. The pervert swiftly arranged himself back in his pants, and stumbling over chairs, high tailed it out of the theater. Rosetta and I laughed so hard we couldn't concentrate on the movie.

When we were able to get more money we would go to the Apollo. Now that was a treat. A show consisted of at least five acts who were the likes of Smokey and the Miracles, The Supremes, Jackie Wilson, Tommy Hunt, James Brown, Marvin Gay, The Marvellettes, Red Foxx, Moms Mabley, and others. During those days, aside from seeing the show you would also see a short movie or cartoon and the band would play and people from the audience were allowed to go on stage to dance. Well one day, I took my skinny (I mean slim) self up to dance. I was wearing a latest style, a short wide skirt that had attached shorts with elastic on the legs.

However, the elastic was not clinging to my thighs, so I looked pitiful but didn't know it. I always liked to dance and did so every chance I got. The Boston Monkey was out at the time and I was doing it to death. I was in my own world and had not noticed the audience laughter. I only realized when I heard Rosetta calling, beckoning me to get off the stage. She was so mad at the audience. If she could, she would have taken each person on one at a time.

The Club ended abruptly one day after Rosetta and one of the girls had a knock down drag out fight at the sisters' house. It was over the girl not paying her dues on a regular basis. Rosetta was the treasurer and expressed her concern about the girl reaping the benefits of belonging to the club, participating in the activities, but not contributing financially. One thing led to another and they fought. They broke a few items in the sisters' house, which caused them to get a beating when their mother came home. After that, everyone agreed the Club should be dissolved.

We were always groping for excitement, entertainment and direction. The later seemed lacking as the adults seemed too busy, trying to make ends meet, to give us time and advice. Actually, we never asked for it because we did not want to impose or get rejected. The kids on the block had so much talent, but did not have the parental support and financial means to cultivate that talent. It would be unfair to cast blame on the parents because they were so involved in trying to survive, in that environment, and provide for their families, that they did not have the time or insight to concentrate on such things as cultivating their children's talents.

Although Ma was not attuned to our individual talents, she did have enough insight to keep us engaged in constructive activities. Each year, Ma sent all of her children who were of age, to camps in rural areas located in Upstate New York. She seized the opportunity to expose us to another environment in which we were able to learn and do things that were not available in our neighborhood. Ma was charged $2.00 for each child's two weeks stay. Although she probably would have loved having us all go to camp at the same time, which would have given her a hiatus from us, that was not possible. The times that we were to go to camp were determined by our ages and the various schedules of the different camps that we attended. Therefore, Rosetta and I never went to camp together. At camp, I was able to touch a cow for the first time and learned that the milk we drank from cartons actually came from cows. Everything was so calm and peaceful in the country environment at camp. There were no sounds of police, fire engines, and ambulance sirens penetrating the darkness of the night and disturbing my sleep. At first it was strange to hear the sounds of crickets singing their songs in the stillness of the night; seeing strange animals like raccoons and skunks foraging outside the cabins; and being able to ask for second helpings of food without being told that it may not be enough for others. Our days were filled with participating in many different activities such as boating, swimming, archery, gardening, hiking, arts and crafts, fishing, horseback riding, softball, volleyball and sitting around campfires singing. At camp, I learned how to set a dinner table and proper table manners. After returning from camp, Rosetta and I would share our camp experiences and complain about not getting merit feathers and awards. For the life of us we could not understand why we were never recognized as good campers, in spite of the fact that we fought at camp, participated in raiding the kitchen after dark, refused to help look for wood for the campfires and refused to participate in activities we did not like. In our minds those were not sufficient reasons to deny us merit awards. We strongly felt that it was difficult adjusting to such a vastly different environment and should have been acknowledged for the adjustments we did make. For instance, although we had one or two fights during the two week period, it was a tremendous improvement over our norm of fighting on a daily basis. Since we did not receive the recognition we felt we deserved, we perceived the camp counselors and administrators as being unfair and prejudice. Year after year we pondered those issues amongst ourselves. It never dawned on us to share our concerns with our parents and they never asked us about our experiences. Perhaps if we had discussed our concerns with Ma, she could have shed some light on our dilemma.

Although we had tons of fun having a big family and living in Harlem, I always felt something was missing. There seemed to live, inside of me, a desire to show and receive affection. We did not display outward affection in my household. Although we all knew that we loved each other, it was never said. To compensate, each year I brought different types of pets home from camp. They were either turtles, frogs or salamanders. I took great pride in caring for my pets, however for some reason, they never lasted long. My siblings would tell me that they got out of the fish bowls and disappeared.

One day, I bought six little chicks from the pet store. That night I put them in a box and placed the box under the stove in the kitchen. When I got up the next morning, there was blood everywhere. A rat had gotten to the chicks and ate three of them. One of the remaining three was visibly petrified. It ran whenever I tried to pick it up and continued to do so even when it became a hen. The tears streamed down my eyes as I cleaned up the blood. Aware of my despair, Daddy helped me clean up the blood. I told him that I did not know what to do because the rat would probably come back that night to eat the rest of my chicks. Lovingly he patted my head and told me that he would take care of it. Daddy got dressed, went out and returned with wood, wire and nails. He went out on the fire escape and built a chicken coop. It wasn't too big and fit comfortably on the fire escape. There was still lots of room left, on the fire escape, for us to play. Daddy was my hero, like Superman he saved the day. He taught me how to feed and care for them. I fed them cooked corn meal and water. I also had to change the paper in the chicken coop each day, which I did without complaining. None of my siblings wanted to help. They thought I was silly bringing in pets that required me to perform additional chores besides the ones I normally had to do each day. Obviously, this created a problem when I went away to camp for two weeks, because when I returned, my chickens were gone. On the fire escape was the empty chicken coop that Daddy had lovingly built for my chickens. Where could they be? Someone was playing a trick on me. I looked under beds, in closets, in boxes and every place I could think of but they were no where to be found. Frantically, I asked everyone what happened to my chickens. Rosetta was the only person who responded to my inquiries. Sadly, with tears in her eyes, she told me that Richie had taken two of them on the roof and wanted to see if they could fly. So those two died in that manner. The other one was given to one of my aunts who cooked it. I was devastated. How could they kill my pets? How could Ma allow that to happen? I was even more devastated to learn that Ma was home when they were killing my chickens. I felt betrayed by my family. No one understood what that meant to me. Daddy had not been home and did not even notice that the chickens were gone. My siblings, with the exception of Rosetta, thought I was crazy reacting the way I did. They did not understand why I was crying, hysterically. Rosetta tried to comfort me but I could tell that she too thought I was over reacting. This was one of many events that caused me to feel alienated and different from the rest of my siblings. Since that day, I felt I could no longer trust my siblings, with the exception of Rosetta. Although I still loved them, I did not like them anymore. That day they took more than my pets away, they took my trust. I later learned that that event affected my trusting people, as I continued with my life.

It seemed my siblings were always against me. Probably

51

because I was always the first one to try new things. I remember when, as the first of my siblings to attend college, I was overjoyed to receive a grant through the SEEK program to attend City College of New York. It was during the late sixties when the civil rights struggle was in full bloom. The struggle for Black people to obtain equal rights was on the minds of us Black college students. I remember taking a Black literature course. We had a project which required us to write poetry that depicted the times. Having read Nikki Giovanni, Sonia Sanchez and other contemporary female poets, I developed a similar style and wanted to share with my family, some of my poetry. So I gathered them all together, including Daddy, and did a poetry reading set to music. They had never experienced anything like that before and it was a complete disaster. Although I was prepared to read a collection of my poems, I was only able to get through one, before all hell broke loose. The poem read as follows:

> Love, Love, Love, wow
> Why not take it?
> Why not take it now?
> Live, Live, Live for today
> For tomorrow, tomorrow
> You may be dead
> Dead, Dead, Dead, Death
> Hell, Hell, Hell, Hell
> Burn you fool for I tell you now
> For you should have loved and lived and
> been proud.

While I read the poem, my family was visibly in shock. When I finished, Richie was the first to comment. He shook his head and said, "see Ma, that's the crap that they teach in college. She would do better getting a full time job and do something useful with herself." Daddy got up and in his loudest voice said, "You child, what kind of language are you learning in that school. I do not want you to use such language around me anymore. That is foolishness." Ma and Vanessa did not say a word, but looked at me in disgust. Nicole had an expression on her face that seemed to say, I'm glad everybody disliked your poem. Gregory and Laura were stretched out laughing on the floor. Kevin seemed to have been contemplating the message to my poem. Rosetta came over to me, as I started to cry, and in a consoling tone said, "that's too heavy for them, they don't understand where you're coming from. Don't pay them any mind, just don't read anymore of your poems to them. Read them to me when we are alone." That was a totally humiliating experience and the last time I ever shared anything related to school with my family. Aside from Rosetta, my family thought I was a fool. They demonstrated no support of me and from that day on, they were critical of just about everything I did.

My family had another opportunity to express their disgust with me when I was arrested during Civil Rights protests at City College. I was the first and only one, of my siblings, to ever be arrested, so when Ma received a call from me while I was still at the precinct, she had no idea what to do. She contacted Richie, Nicole and Daddy. They were present, at the arraignment, along with my College Counselor, who was shocked to hear that I had been arrested. The counselor knew that I hardly ever hung around the school because I always had to go to work. When I was released at 1:00 am, they were shocked to see my badly swollen jaw and battered body. A racist police officer had beaten me up pretty badly while calling me "stupid Nigger." I was laid up in bed for more than a week as a result of that beating. The charges against me were eventually dismissed, but the family never stopped talking about how stupid I was to have gotten into that situation. To them, the civil rights movement was something to watch on TV; it was not supposed to come into our home. Their thinking was like many others, who thought of the fight for civil rights as something that they gave lip service to and supported morally but not to get involved with physically. They just didn't understand and I was tired of trying to enlighten them. Although Daddy had read and listened to Black speakers on 125th Street talk about the inequities that existed during those times, he evidently did not bargain on any of his children actually marching to bring attention to the need for change. My family considered me an outsider in my way of thinking. I felt alienated and rejected by my family. Rosetta was my only support. She understood me and could be depended on whenever life was confusing and people proved unreliable.

MA

Born in 1923, the first of five children, Ma was light brown skinned, thin, with long jet black hair. As the oldest child, she had the responsibility of taking care of her four younger siblings while her mother, a domestic worker, worked in New Rochelle, New York caring for two white children. Grandma would leave her home each morning at approximately 5:00am and not return until 8:00pm, Monday thru Friday and sometimes on Saturdays. Ma had to wake up her siblings, prepare breakfast, make sure they were dressed properly and send them off to school. When the two younger children were not of school age, she would feed them, make sure they used the bathroom, put them back to bed and instruct them not to get out of the bed while she was at school. She had to leave them in the bed, unsupervised, until she returned home for lunch. She would prepare lunch, feed the two younger children, have them use the bathroom again, put them back in the bed and again instruct them not to get out of the bed until she returned home at 3:00pm.

Then she would prepare dinner, feed the children, bathe them and prepare the clothes for the next day. This happened day in and day out. She often told us, with longing in her voice, how she felt like she never had a childhood. As we got older, she would sometimes say "I'm so tired of raising children." Now, I realize what she must have been feeling. It makes me sad to think about her childhood that was consumed with adult type of responsibilities. She never experienced playing childhood games, having friends and, later as a teenager, experiencing the joys of innocent courtship.

At the age of eighteen, Ma was a senior at Central Commercial High School and a highly skilled typist who was extended an offer to work for a federal agency in Washington, D.C., upon graduation. However, one day when traveling home after school, a 27 year-old married man approached Ma. He was very handsome with smooth soft dark black skin, jet black curly hair, a wide grin which revealed beautifully aligned white teeth and cool words that eventually charmed the pants right off the very sheltered, gullible, emotionally starved teenager. After several brief sexual encounters, Ma got pregnant. When she informed Mr. Cool, he relocated to California with his family.

One day, eleven years later, Richie came upstairs with two dollars and told Ma that a man, who said he was his father, gave him the money. Outraged, Ma took the money from Richie and proceeded down the block where she found Mr. Cool. She threw the money in his face, told him to take it and shove it up his ass and warned him never to approach her son again.

While pregnant with Richie, Ma had to drop out of school which ended her opportunity to work in Washington, D.C. In those days, pregnant girls were not allowed to stay in school. Needless to say, Grandma was disappointed as she hoped Ma would make something of herself and not have to struggle the way she did. She never wanted any of her children to have to clean white people's floors or take care of white children, as she had because of her lack of education and other skills. Ma was determined not to do domestic work. In fact, she often told us stories of being approached by white women asking her if she was available to do domestic work. Appalled, she would ask them if she had "work needed" written across her forehead.

Ma met and married Daddy who was tall, distinguished looking, debonair, and 17 years her senior. He had been married twice before with no children. He had a quiet presence, a charming smile and a look that clearly stated, I don't take any bullshit. He had a history of being a boxer, a lover and a gambler. Draw Poker was his game, which he played every weekend. Although Daddy lived with us, we hardly saw him and on rare occasions,held brief conversations with him. He was a mystery to us, coming in and out of our lives. Ma said that he had a gift for reading cards which he demonstrated one night when a friend of Ma's and her husband came to visit. When Ma brought up the topic of Daddy's gift of card reading, the skeptical man challenged Daddy to read his cards. At first Daddy refused and tried to change the subject. The man was persistent and insisted that

Every Heart Knows Its Own Sorrow

Daddy read his cards. When Daddy continued to decline, the man called Daddy a liar and some other derogatory names. Angry at the man's insulting manner, Daddy accepted the challenge and proceeded to read the cards. He told the man about events that occurred at his work place, his family situation and when a queen of hearts appeared, Daddy stopped reading the cards. The man insisted that Daddy continue, but Daddy warned him that it was not a good idea. When the man became insulting again, Daddy resumed reading the cards and told the man about the woman that he was having an affair with. Outraged, the man stood up to physically attack Daddy, but decided to leave instead when he saw Daddy take a boxing stance. Daddy never read cards in our home again and Ma stopped talking about his special gift. However, that episode did not stop Daddy from playing poker. We never really knew how often he won because he never told us. We just did what Ma told us to do every Sunday morning after he fell asleep. We would take his pants off of the hook next to the door in their room, and empty the pockets. Daddy had to know that we were doing this. He probably deliberately left a certain amount of money in the pockets, knowing that we were going to take it. With that money, Ma would give us our collection for church and the next day send us food shopping.

Food shopping was always a chore. Because money was always limited, Ma had to search for sales to make ends meet. She was an expert at it. We had to travel long distances to shop, sometimes going to two and three stores in different parts of town for the sales. We hated traveling such long

58

distances, sometimes going to one store for bread and then another store, six blocks away for meat. The chore of actually doing the shopping was passed down to Rosetta and me when the three older siblings started working after school. Ma played the numbers and whenever she won, Rosetta and I knew we had to go on another journey to the stores. Ma had "a system" for figuring out the numbers. Of course, the system was not scientific or accurate, but it made her happy to believe it worked, so we did not dispute it. Rosetta was Ma's favorite to play her numbers because a few of the number runners liked Rosetta and would pay her off even when Ma did not hit the numbers. They never got fresh with Rosetta. They knew her reputation for fighting, so they were content to hold brief polite conversations with her and satisfied themselves with her polite "thank you."

Ma and Daddy frequently had arguments, usually about money. Because Daddy gambled so much and evidently lost a lot of money, he was not consistently contributing financially to our support, which left the burden on Ma to make ends meet. Ma would often get angry, pack us all up and move in with Grandma. This happened at least five times. The last time, Ma allowed Vanessa and Nicole to remain in the Bronx with Grandma after Ma and the rest of us moved back to live with Daddy on 7th Avenue. Vanessa and Nicole were in Junior High School and Ma did not want to interrupt their education. When the school year ended they moved back home to finish the ninth grade. The last time that Ma moved in with Grandma, Grandma shook her head and asked Ma when was she going to stop interrupting our lives by moving us back and forth? Later, Ma explained to us when she moved back with Daddy, if anyone had to move again, it would be him.

I always had a very special relationship with Daddy. He was an avid reader and would allow me to get in bed with him and watch him read. He read the Black Muslim newspaper, the Daily News, and a variety of books by black authors. We never talked about the books. I was content just being near Daddy. Sometimes Ma would make me leave even when Daddy would say "Dot, leave the child alone." When I was four and five years old I remember going under Daddy's coat whenever he came home. Holding onto his leg, he carried me in that manner, laughing all the way to his room. I thought my father was the most handsome, proudest, strongest, and most interesting man in the world. So when I was fourteen years old and he had to move out of the house, I was devastated. One day as I was returning home from school I saw Daddy being escorted, by two cops, out of the building and into a police car. Frantically, I ran over to him, crying and demanding that the cops let my father loose. When he was seated in the car, one police officer closed the door and told me that everything was going to be fine. I looked at Daddy and he said to me in a solemn broken voice, "Carol, don't cry. I'll be alright. Go upstairs and tell your mother that I am sorry." Then the cops took Daddy away. When I went upstairs and saw Ma's face, I almost fainted. Never had I seen even a scratch on Ma, but now she had, what seemed to me, a huge purplish knot on her forehead. She was sitting in the living room, on the sofa, weeping. I felt helpless and confused. My parents had a fight and my hero, Daddy, had hurt Ma. My world felt like it came to an end. This could not be happening. I wanted to embrace Ma and tell her that everything was going to be alright, but in my heart, I knew things would never be the same. I gave her Daddy's message, but I knew she wasn't listening, so I kept my distance on the sofa and continued to sob with Ma. Ma did not press charges, but Daddy had to move out of the apartment. Shortly after the incident, Ma allowed him to visit us, but they never got back together. Although what he did to Ma was unforgivable, I continued to love Daddy, even when I became an adult and he died; alone in his apartment, on his knees in a praying position, facing the East.

After Daddy moved out of the house, we had to go on welfare. I remember the demeaning manner in which the social workers would talk to Ma. It angered me to see my mother being spoken to in such a disrespectful manner, sometimes by women much younger than she. One day a social worker came to the house and lined all of the children up in front of her, and asked us what did we want to be when we grew up? Nicole said she wanted to be a teacher. Rosetta said, a mother. Gregory said, a fireman. Kevin was not sure. When I answered that I wanted to become a lawyer, the social worker told me that I would never become a lawyer and I should think about being something different. Her response to me was shocking. All my life I wanted to be a lawyer and here was this disrespectful, nasty white woman coming into my home, degrading the entire family and telling me I could not be what I wanted to be. That was appalling.

Every Heart Knows Its Own Sorrow

I looked at Ma hoping she would tell that women off and demand that she leave our house, but Ma only bowed her head in a helpless manner. I felt sorry for Ma. Although I did not understand what was going on and who that woman was, I knew that Ma was hurting. Until that day, my exposure to white people was limited to my teachers, store owners and cops. Besides my teachers, I had never held a conversation with a white person until that day. If that is what they say to children, then I made up my mind that I would be careful not to speak to them, if I could help it.

Unfortunately, I had to speak with my ninth grade guidance counselor to complete my application for high school. During our meeting, she asked me what I wanted to do when I grew up. Earlier that year, a Black female lawyer who was the New York State Senator, Constance Baker Motley (who later became Manhattan Borough President and the first Black woman federal judge) had visited the school and gave an inspiring message to the students about setting goals and following our dreams. I was so inspired by her speech that it canceled out what that social worker had said to me. Now when my guidance counselor asked me, I said with a great deal of confidence, "a lawyer." To my surprise, she said the same thing that the social worker had said, except she suggested that I consider becoming a secretary. I could not believe my ears. Was this a conspiracy to kill my spirit? When I insisted that I knew what I wanted to do and which school I wanted to attend, because it had a special program that would prepare me for college, she insisted that I go to another high school that would prepare me to become a secretary. With that, she dismissed me.

In tears I went to my home room class. My teacher, a black women, who was also my algebra teacher, spoke to me after dismissing the class. I told her about the incident. Without any signs of amazement about the issue, she asked me the name of the school that I wanted to attend and told me to tell my mother to go with me, on the first day of classes, to the school that I wanted to attend. She told me that my application will not be at that school, but my records will be. Sure enough, we did what she said and I was placed in the college preparatory program. That teacher was bent on making sure that I succeeded in getting into the school of my choice. She had always been encouraging to the students and took a special interest in students, like me, who worked hard and excelled academically. It seemed as though a battle had been waged involving White people, that I had encountered, who were bent on killing my spirit and drive to succeed and the caring Black people, that I encountered, who had to work even harder to save me from becoming disillusioned. I will always be grateful to that teacher and have, in my professional life, followed her example and tried to do good deeds for others.

When we went on welfare, Ma had to work even harder to make ends meet. I remember seeing her on the floor looking under beds, pulling back chairs and looking under the chair cushions for change that might have fallen. Some nights, through an opening in the french door curtains, I would see Ma gazing out the window and up to the sky, as if she was wishing on a star. Other times I would see her kneeling at the foot of the bed with her hands, palms together, praying. In spite of being alone and having to bare the burden of raising so many children, she never let us see her cry. Somehow, things worked out. She managed the meager welfare allotment wisely. We never went to bed hungry. She knew how to make ends meet by shopping and cooking wisely. She cooked soups, stews, chicken wings, meat loaf, ox tails, rice, potatoes, spaghetti, cabbage, greens, string beans, corn and other economical meals that could, as Ma would say, "stretch." She baked delicious biscuits, yeast rolls and cinnamon buns. Before going to bed, we always had a snack to eat. On Sundays she always cooked fricassee chicken, peas and rice and a vegetable. The amazing thing was that, not only did she have enough to feed us, but there was also always enough to feed anyone who visited.

Although Rosetta and I hated to go to the food depot, where they distributed surplus food to the economically disadvantaged, Ma insisted that we go. Again, as with the hand outs of toys, we encountered having to stand on long lines for hours in the cold, waiting to be handed powdered milk, flour, corn meal, powdered eggs, beans, potted meat, shortening, butter, rice and cheese. It was embarrassing to see people passing by staring at us as we stood for hours, in the cold, on long lines waiting to be allowed inside to get the food. It was embarrassing when we entered the block and our friends saw the welfare food. Rosetta and I would try to disguise the food by putting the items in laundry bags and placing a few grocery items on top of the cart that squeaked from the weight of the welfare food, but everyone still knew what we had in the laundry bags. We were fooling no one, but covering up the food made us feel better. When I became an adult, I prayed that my children would never have to experience the humiliation of being treated as less than human beings for any reason, but especially because of being financially disadvantaged. We did not want to be without money, as I believe no one wants to be, so why should people be treated in an inhuman manner because of their financial shortcomings?

Although we were economically disadvantaged, we were happy. We did not allow our economic condition to dominate our general well being. So we found ways of compensating and being happy. Our house was always filled with love, and the sounds of music and laughter. On Fridays and Saturdays we always had company; something was always happening at Ma's house. Often, especially when Ma was broke, she would sell dinners to the people in the apartment downstairs who were playing cards and to the patrons of the bar in the building. They loved when Ma did that West Indian cooking. They clamored for her peas and rice, smothered chicken, pig feet, potato salad, collard greens, cabbage, biscuits and ginger beer. Rosetta and I were responsible for delivering the dinners. We didn't complain because occasionally we received tips.

Ma's house was the place where our cool neighbors knew they could come to be in the company of nice people who treated them with respect. Some came to talk to Ma about their problems. They knew that they would receive compassionate, kind words. Others came to eat, drink, be merry and forget about their everyday worries. We had one of the few stereos on the block, so everyone wanted to hear the wonderful music. Our neighbor, Miss Blair, in the next building would open and lean out of her window, that was adjacent to ours, to hear the music and see the dancing. Gregory, Kevin and two of their friends had organized themselves into a band. Gregory was the drummer and vocalist, Kevin played the bass guitar and sang vocals, the other two guys, Ronny and Ben played lead guitar and keyboard. They were pretty good. They were our block's band. Mrs. Kates children were excellent singers and from time to time would come down to our house and sing with the band. They used to rock the house. They really sounded good together. We would party from sun down to sun up. There were never any fights, arguments or inappropriate behavior. Everyone respected Miss Dot (that's what they called Ma). I especially loved the times when my aunts came over. They loved to party and did so regularly. I was the self proclaimed DJ and bartender. I knew what everyone drank and would intentionally fix potent drinks that would get my aunts high. Then I would put on their favorite records and watch them perform by dancing and crying over lost loves. They loved to see me perform a comical dance I did to the record *He's a rebel*. I would dance around and swing my legs as though they were wooden legs, first the left one and then the right. It was a pretty funny dance and I loved making them laugh. The joy, laughter, and bonding that took place during those gatherings, provided us with temporary relief from the pressures of our environment. Those are the memories that we all hold dear to our hearts which cause the bonds between us to remain strong.

Much to my father's dismay, my aunts and Godmother taught Rosetta and me how to play poker. So when we were not partying on Saturday nights, Rosetta and I would often play poker. We were the only two of my parents' children who played poker. Daddy never wanted any of his children to play cards, but we learned and played anyway. Playing cards with my aunts, Godmother and their friends was wonderful. Most of their friends worked at various city jobs, so at least once a month, we were able to afford to play cards with them. When Rosetta and I became old enough to work, we always held jobs after school, therefore we had money to play cards. When we got older we became pretty good friends with that crowd. We would travel to their houses and stay up all night playing cards. They were very nice people who showed us how to play hard core poker. Rosetta and I eventually got so good at poker that they refused to play cards with us anymore.

On some Saturday mornings, Grandma would come over. Grandma was a tall, robust, chinky eyed, brown skinned women who spoke with a strong West Indian accent. The Matriarch of the family, she came to New York from the West Indies by herself at the age of twenty-two. Without having any close relatives here, she met and married my Grandfather. Their relationship was rocky because he, like my father, was a gambler. My Grandfather was also from Barbuda, however he was not tall and handsome. He was light skinned, medium height, heavy build with big bulging eyes and a balding head. They had five children together, but Grandma was left with the burden of raising the children alone, when he left shortly after their last child was born. He did not contribute to the financial support of the family, because of his gambling problem, so he had to leave.

It was difficult working and raising five children alone. Being unskilled, Grandma worked as a domestic, earning meager wages. Although she wrote and sent her parents money, food, clothing and other items, she was never able to save enough money to return home before they died. So once she left her parents in Antigua, she never saw them again. After her children were grown, she was finally able to return home for a visit. She visited her parents' grave sites and spent hours there crying and praying.

We loved those Saturday mornings when Grandma visited. We would get up early to eat and listen to Grandma's wonderful stories. She talked about her home, family and friends in the West Indies and shared interesting tales about her father, who loved to fight. It was always quite obvious that Grandma missed her parents and siblings. She always talked about them and shared stories about her childhood. She also made us aware that we got our knack for fighting from her father who was known, in his village, for fighting. One of the stories, that she told, was about the time a man from the village stole one of her father's goats. When Great Grandpa found out, he fought the man, knocked him out and proceeded to knock out all of the man's finger nails, with a stone. She said that her father always told his children not to start trouble, but if someone does something to you, then get him back. Grandma also told us never to do anything that we would be sorry for later. She told us to never accept apologies, because if a person didn't want to do something to hurt you, then he would not have done it in the first place. Her rationale was plain and simple and her philosophy was "think before you act."

On those Saturday morning visits to our house, Grandma brought with her lox, bagels, cream cheese and pumpernickel bread. Obviously, she acquired a taste for that food from working for Jews. She explained how it was coming to this country, the hardships she endured, and the friends who helped her. The overriding message to her stories was the strength of the family, and she stressed that we must always stick together. Unfortunately, I did not feel that I could depend on my siblings to stick with me, given the way they rejected me in the past. However, I never shared those feelings with Grandma because I did not want to disappoint her.

Most of all, we loved going to Grandma's house. She was always in the kitchen, cooking, washing clothes, ironing or doing something. Very rarely did Grandma leave the kitchen when we visited her. She loved waiting on us. When we would spend the night, Grandma would bathe each of us, regardless of our ages. While bathing us she explained how to properly bathe, all the while scrubbing us with a scrub brush, behind our necks, our elbows, knees, knuckles, backs, feet, and everywhere. When she got through with us we were cleannnnn. It was heaven sleeping in Grandma's beds; she starched her sheets by using the cooked starch. All washing was done by hand using the scrub board. Even when Ma insisted that we take the clothes to the laundromat, whenever we stayed over at Grandma's house, she would still hand wash the clothes when we returned from the laundromat. Then, she would show us the startling amount of dirt that came out of the clothes that we had washed at the laundromat. Everything in Grandma's house smelled fresh and clean. Some of my most restful sleeping took place in Grandma's house.

Ma got her strength to survive from Grandma. Much to Grandma's delight, Ma never gave up and always inspired us to get a good education. Although she found herself with the responsibility of raising eight children with virtually little help, Ma managed to do so and also pursued her goal of going back to school and receiving a high school diploma. She even attended college at the age of fifty-five. Whenever she got the opportunity, she volunteered at community organizations by typing and answering phones. Although her situation seemed overwhelming, she never allowed herself to be overwhelmed. She always stressed education to us. We had to study after school and were not allowed to go downstairs to play on school days. I always needed extra remedial help in reading, which I received at school. None of my sisters and brothers knew that I had difficulty reading. Whenever I did my homework and had problems reading, I would us my skills of manipulation to get Rosetta or Nicole to read to me. They loved to read and I gave them the opportunity to show off their reading skills. When we became adults, they were amazed to learn that I had a reading problem as a child. I was so skillful at hiding it that even Ma did not know about my reading problem.

That problem did not hamper me from being the first person in my entire family to graduate from college and graduate school. I remember not wanting to attend my college graduation, but did so after mentioning it to Ma and seeing the disappointment in her face. I then thought about Grandma, who when I was eleven, took me with her to one of the homes that she cleaned. At the time, I had no idea why she took me with her. It was a Jewish lady's apartment located in Manhattan, on East 95th Street. I had never been to any apartments in that neighborhood and had no idea that an apartment could be so pretty. It was lavishly furnished with expensive plush carpets and elaborately decorated chairs. There were lots of mirrors and paintings of country scenes on the walls. I was amazed to see such beautiful things. Grandma would not allow me to help her, instead, she instructed me to sit in a corner in the kitchen. All she wanted me to do was watch her clean. When the resident of the apartment came home, without saying a word, she glanced at me and proceeded into her bedroom. I remember thinking how rude she was. Didn't she know that it was polite to say hello when entering a room and seeing someone there. It wasn't until I looked in Ma's face when I told her about not wanting to attend my graduation and remembered watching Grandma clean those floors, that I understood why she took me with her. When I walked across that stage at graduation, I proudly accepted that degree, for Grandma and Ma.

RELATIONSHIPS

The tangled web

INNOCENCE

When I became a "young lady," I had no idea what was happening to me. For a week, I was sick at home with stomach aches and a fever. Although I was sick, I felt quite special being home with Ma and Daddy all by myself. I remember hearing Daddy ask Ma what was wrong with me. They were laying in bed talking and Ma's reply was "it's nothing but she's becoming a young lady." "What the heck did that mean?" I thought to myself. It seemed to me that she should at least let me in on the secret. I thought I was a young lady already. What did being in pain have to do with becoming a young lady? Little did I know then, that for many years to come, pain would be a constant presence in my adulthood.

When my period finally came later that week, Ma showed me how to put on a Kotex and instructed me "not to play with boys" because I could now become pregnant. Well, there was no more playing with the boys downstairs. I even refused to play my favorite game "Red Rover, Red Rover" because we usually played that game with the boys and I did not want to get pregnant. Clearly, Ma should have taken more time and been more specific with what she meant by "not playing with boys." I obviously took her words literally, and as a result they ended my childhood pleasures. It wasn't until I spent time with the first guy I dated, that I realized what Ma meant.

His name was Robby. I met him one day when I went to meet my sister, Nicole, at her job in the garment district. Robby was loading dresses on a truck and started calling after me. I thought it was flattering that an older guy would find me attractive enough to try to get my attention. I was so naive. At fourteen years old, although still slim, my bra size was 34C. I am sure that's what he was calling after, however, I did not realize it. Big breasts ran in my family on my father's side. Cousin Ester had to be at least a 40FF. When Nicole came downstairs, she introduced us. He seemed like a nice guy and Nicole said he was decent. He lived in Brooklyn and was a senior in high school. His skin was dark and he had broad shoulders, big lips and short front teeth. I did not find him attractive, but I did like his dark skin and broad shoulders.

When he asked me to go to the movies with him, I accepted because I wanted to brag to my friends that my first date was going to be with an older guy. I gave him my telephone number and he called me that night and every night until our date. His conversations were cool. He had plans of finishing high school and joining the Air Force. That impressed me because I never knew anyone who went into the Air Force. The Air Force seemed to be a more prestigious branch of the armed forces. The guys in my neighborhood who went into the service usually joined the Army.

Our first date went well. He picked me up at the house and of course was scrutinized by the entire family, however the only opinion I could not wait to hear was Rosetta's. Rosetta was highly critical and I trusted her judgment. We went down to 42nd Street, ate dinner, and went to the movies. That was a real treat for me because seldom had I eaten in a restaurant. Ma and Daddy couldn't afford to take us out to eat. Occasionally, Daddy took me and Rosetta to the Chinese restaurant, but that was very rare. Robby brought me back home and I gave him a peck on the cheek and thanked him for a wonderful evening. I was an avid movie watcher and gave him the lines that I heard in so many movies. I thought that was the thing to do. I was scared to death and, quite frankly, did not know what else to say or do. It worked. He called me when he got home and thanked me for a great time. I didn't know whether he was lying or not about having a great time. No one had ever told me that they enjoyed my company, so for him to say that he had a great time was somewhat unbelievable. I could not wait until the next morning to tell Rosetta about my date. That night, I dreamed about our date and how we walked together holding hands. I felt so secure with him since he was big and strong. He looked like he could protect both of us. It was comfortable, when traveling on the subway with him, feeling certain that no one would mess with us. The next morning when Rosetta woke up, she expressed her opinion of him by saying that he was ugly and I could do better. Disappointed with her opinion, I decided that she was just dealing with his physical appearance and if she got to know him she would like him too.

We continued to talk on the phone each night, sometimes for hours. Then he came over one evening to visit. We watched TV and talked. As the evening progressed, he placed his arm around my shoulders and drew me close to him. I tried to ignore him but it felt comfortable. I relaxed and enjoyed being engulfed in his strong broad shoulders. Of course, I could not totally relax because my younger siblings would come in and out of the room, giggling like fools. Daddy did not like the idea of me having company and was just as bad as my siblings. The only difference, he was not giggling. After my father left for work and the younger kids were in bed, Robby made his move. He turned me around and in one swift movement was kissing me. Then, I felt his tongue in my mouth and my lips being drawn into his mouth. It felt like a vacuum was pulling my face into his mouth. I could not believe that he was so nasty as to put his tongue in my mouth and my mouth in his mouth. I abruptly pulled away from him and ran into the bathroom. Frantically, I brushed my teeth, rinsed my mouth and stood looking at myself in the mirror for at least five minutes trying to figure out how to get rid of him. Finally, I decided, just tell him to leave. Bravely, I re-entered the living room and, in a theatrical voice, said "Robby, I would like you to leave." He tried to say something, but I was not listening. I politely opened the door and said "leave." Hanging his head, as if ashamed, he proceeded out of the door and said " Carol, I did not mean to offend you, I'm sorry." Without any hesitation, I closed the door in his face.

Totally bewildered, I went back into the bathroom and started to cry. That was the first time I had kissed a guy and I did not like it. In the movies it seemed so nice. I had no idea that kissing meant putting your tongue in the other person's mouth. I wondered whether everyone did that. I couldn't ask my buddy Rosetta because she had never kissed anyone. I wanted to ask Nicole, but we did not have a close relationship and I thought she might laugh at me. My oldest sister would probably lie to me and I dare not ask Ma, because she might think the whole thing disgusting. So, I didn't say anything to anyone that night. Rosetta knew something was wrong and tried to pry it out of me, but I remembered the last time I confided in her about a girl and a guy, and thought it best not to chance telling her. I didn't want to end up out on the fire escape again. I felt so alone, with no one I could talk to about my concerns.

Going to school the next day, I felt guilty and thought that everyone could tell what I did last night. It was hard for me to concentrate on school work. I distanced myself from my friends at school, feeling dirty and used. Then one of my friends, Vern, approached me and asked what was the matter. I shook my head and said, "nothing." She persisted, saying, "Carol, you are always so lively and happy, why are you so sad today." Vern was one of the fast girls in the school. She was very popular with the boys and was always talking about going out with different boys. I always envied her popularity with the boys, but had no idea why she was so popular. Since she was experienced with dealing with boys, I broke down and told her. She sucked her teeth and said "Is that why you're upset?" Vern then explained to me that it was fun to kiss boys and that tonguing was the way people kissed. She encouraged me to see him again, told me not to worry about anything and suggested that I try to relax and enjoy it the next time.

Well, I was relieved to hear that people regularly did this. I felt better and even accepted Robby's call that evening. We talked about my reaction and I explained to him that he was the first guy that I ever kissed. That must have boosted his ego because he got very excited and pleaded with me to allow him to visit me again. After a few weeks of talking on the phone, I allowed him to visit me again. This time we played records and talked. I was always able to keep a conversation going. As the evening drew on, Daddy went to work and the kids went to sleep. Robby made his advances again. This time I allowed him to kiss me, but I still did not like it. His kisses were hard and they hurt my lips. I tried to do what Vern said, relax and enjoy it. I even put my tongue in his mouth when I got the chance to. He was so busy putting his tongue in my mouth that it was difficult finding the opportunity to reciprocate. I guess Robby was pleased with my reaction because he hurriedly unzipped his pants and took out his penis. Well, I thought I was surprised before, but that hadn't come close to my astonishment this time. I had never seen a grown man's penis before. The only penises I saw were my little brothers' when I had to bathe them. But this was something totally different. This penis was real big and hard with all this hair all around the bottom of it. It looked mean and fierce, like it was angry and wanted to get back at me. I stared at it for a long time, not able to move. It reminded me of a big black snake with a big head. I guess Robby took my staring at it as approval for him to make further advances. He then took my hand and put it on that big black head. It seemed to grow even bigger and more fierce. It felt like a hard cushion, meaning, it was hard but not rock hard. It seemed to have a life of its own. It moved by itself and seemed to beckon to me. When I finally got myself together, I stood up and told him to put that back in his pants and leave. He became angry and called me a big tease. I had no idea what he meant and didn't care. All I wanted him to do was leave and never come back. While scrubbing my hands in the bathroom, I vowed that I would never allow him in my home again.

Now, who could I possibly tell this to. There was absolutely no one. The lonely, isolated feeling returned and I knew that I had to bear this alone. I was definitely understanding what Ma meant when she said, do not play with boys anymore. After that experience, seeing what boys had in their pants, I definitely did not want to play with them anymore.

When I returned to school, I tried to act like my normal self in hopes of not attracting Vern's attention. I did not, under any circumstances, want to have another conversation with her about boys. If she thought that whole scene was fun, then I wanted nothing to do with her kind of fun. After that experience I began to see boys in a different way. From my limited experience and given what Vern had shared with me, it seemed boys wanted to do things to girls that I personally was not ready to start doing. Although I had no idea what else Robby wanted to do with his penis besides have me hold it, there was a nagging thought that he probably wanted to do something else. Life started to become more complicated. Why did I have to become a young lady and start dating? It was painful. Innocence is what I wanted to return to, but innocence lost could never be recaptured.

EMBRACED

The excitement of the upcoming wedding filled the April air. Nicole was getting married and I was the maid of honor. She was marrying her boyfriend of two years. The wedding was taking place one day before Nicole's eighteenth birthday. Ma was becoming quite proficient in organizing her girls' weddings. Vanessa was married the year before in a rather quickly planned, however, beautiful wedding. They both wore beautiful white gowns but each completely different in style, which reflected their different personalities. Vanessa's gown was lace with a square neck and a form fitting top with clinging long lace sleeves. The skirt of the gown was lavishly decorated with layers of lace and under it was a rather wide petticoat. Nicole's gown was made of satin. It had a plunging neckline, long form fitting sleeves, and a moderately flowing skirt with a long train. Both Vanessa and Nicole married men from Barbuda, the same island where my father was born. I could not blame them for liking Barbudan men because they were absolutely handsome. Many of them were tall with beautiful smooth skin and bright white teeth. There were plenty of them at those weddings. I was not quite ready to flirt at Vanessa's wedding, since I was trying to recover from the shock of the Robby ordeal, but by the time Nicole got married, I had matured a bit more and was ready to party. By all accounts, I did just that. I tried my best to entertain all those fine young men at the wedding. I had never been anywhere where there were so many good looking single men. It was heaven. I danced every dance with someone different. I was the hostess with the mostess, but was careful not to give them the impression that I wanted to do anything more than dance.

That wedding was the beginning of many fun filled weekends at Nicole's house. We had less parties at Ma's house and more at Nicole's. Nicole's husband, Tyson, would invite his friends over to his house on most Saturday nights. The guys were so fine, polite and fun loving, so Rosetta and I would also go over there on Saturdays. We had lots of fun talking, playing table games, dancing and just spending good clean time together. Of course, some of the guys tried to rap to us and we enjoyed the attention. Rosetta actually went out on dates with a few of them, but none ever developed into anything serious because they were not intellectually challenging enough for her.

Nicole remained close to Ma, even after her marriage. In fact, she came over to the house almost every day. When she had children, they stayed at our house Monday thru Friday while Nicole attended college. Ma said that Nicole's children needed to stay at our house to allow Nicole time to be home and concentrate on her school work. The fact that Rosetta and I were also in college and needed to study never crossed Ma's mind. Her only concern was that Nicole needed to do well in school. Nicole's two children would be at our house making noise, inhibiting our ability to study, so we had to be inconvenienced and study in the library. That was just another example of Ma's favoritism towards Nicole. In spite of those obstacles, Rosetta successfully graduated, with honors, from Fordham University with a Master's degree in Education at the age of twenty-two. At the age of twenty-three, she was teaching at John Jay College for Criminal Justice and has committed her professional life to helping teenage parents receive their high school diplomas.

In October of the same year that Nicole got married, I attended one of my cousin's wedding. It wasn't as exciting as Nicole's wedding; the music was alright, but there weren't as many attractive young men. As I was sitting at a table facing a flight of steps leading to the outside exit, I glanced up at the door and saw the finest looking young man I had ever seen in my life. As he descended the steps, our eyes met and I heard bells ringing in my head. Nothing else existed. We were the only two people in the whole wide world. I was spellbound and so was he. It was like a fairy tale. He was my knight in shining armor and my gallant prince charming all rolled up in one. He was six feet three inches tall and slim, with cocoa dark brown skin and beautiful white teeth. Without uttering a word he approached me and extended his hand, and without hesitation, I took it and we danced for the rest of the evening. Our bodies swayed together in unison to the rhythmic Calypso music. While dancing to slow tunes, I felt his eager body holding me tightly, clinging to me as if his life depended on me saving him. We were totally engrossed in each other and I knew that he was going to be my husband.

Although I was head over heels in love with Shelton, I was cautious. The memory of the Robby ordeal was still fresh in my mind. So I decided to take it slow. We talked on the phone for hours each night but I refused to let him visit me. It wasn't until my sixteenth birthday that I relented and allowed him to take me out. He was eighteen, an immigrant from Barbuda. Yes, another Barbudan man. It seemed we all were destined to be with Barbudan men. We did not mind because, aside from being extremely handsome, they were respectful, polite and hard working men.

Our families knew each other, in fact we were distant relatives on my father's side. We became very good friends. I avoided being alone with him to discourage any romantic situations. He was patient for about six months, but then started to devise plans for us to spend time alone with each other. I resisted for as long as I felt I could without running the risk of losing him. We went to parties together, the movies, bowling, amusement parks, Nicole's house, everywhere I could think of where other people were around. If all else failed, I would put the music on at my house and everyone would start coming. Shelton started to get tired of not having exclusive time with me, and I felt he was starting to get involved with someone else, but he denied it.

By and by, I gradually allowed our relationship to become

more intimate. I had to consciously try to forget Robby and allow myself to get romantically involved with Shelton. To my surprise, Shelton did not kiss like Robby. He was more tender and compassionate. Although he was also into tongue kissing, the way he did it did not seem imposing. In fact, I found myself enjoying kissing Shelton. I got so good at it that I started showing him a thing or two. Since my ordeal with Robby, I attended health education classes and learned some things about sex and the male body. So, I was not appalled when Shelton's penis became hard in his pants. Unlike Robby, he did not just whip it out. He gradually worked up to that. We kissed for a while, then started petting and then he asked me if I wanted to see it. By this time, after feeling it in his pants for so long, I was curious about how it looked. I wondered whether it looked like Robby's, so I said yes. He gingerly took it out, all the while saying how much he loved me and wanted to get closer to me. He was saying that he wanted me to be his girl. No one had ever said those things to me. TO BE HIS GIRL. I felt so close to Shelton, protected and loved, so when I finally looked at his penis, it was not frightening. I was intrigued by it. Although it seemed to throb and move like Robby's, it did not have that fierce look to it. They were both about the same size but Robby's was fatter. Shelton's was more appealing to me. Maybe because it was not the first one that I had seen. Or maybe it was the manner in which he introduced it to me. Or maybe because I loved him. Whatever the reason, I liked looking at it. It felt good to the touch. I explored it and he seemed to enjoy my touch. He coaxed me into squeezing it and at the same time moving my hand up and down. That gave him even more pleasure. I knew he enjoyed it because he made moaning sounds and pleaded with me not to stop. I was happy to bring him pleasure and that excited me. In his excitement, he began caressing my breasts and rubbing the nipples making them hard. I began to experience a strange warm excitement in the lower part of my stomach. This caused me to moan as well. Soon Shelton unbuttoned by blouse, took out one of my breasts and started sucking the nipple. I felt like an explosion erupted in my panties. What was happening to me? I pulled away from him, put my breast back in my bra, told him to put his penis back in his pants and stop. My whole body was shaking. I put my hands over my face and started to cry. Shelton took me in his arms, while rocking me, explained that it was natural to feel what I was feeling and that it was okay. Again, he told me that he loved me and wanted me to be his girl. I had no idea what to do. Should I tell him to leave and never come back, like I had told Robby? But I felt differently towards Shelton. I really liked him. In fact, I loved him and wanted him in my life. Life was becoming more complicated. I assured him that I would be alright, but he should leave and call me the next day. Observing how upset and confused I was, Shelton gave me a tender kiss, told me that he loved me and left.

I knew that I was in over my head and needed to talk to someone. Not having anyone else to talk to, I asked Nicole about sex, and much to my surprise she was very open to discussing it with me. The first thing she said was that I should read books about sex. She suggested *Fanny Hill* and gave me her copy of the book. Nicole really surprised me when she confessed to have been reading about sex for a long time. She said "girl, all those books I was reading when I was younger, most of them were about sex, why do you think I read so much?" As she was telling me about her sex books, I remembered that they always had book covers on them. Imagine that, all along Ma thought she was the great brain, reading about the wonders of the world, when all she was doing was reading about sex. I'm sure, if Vanessa would have known that, she would have been an avid reader also. When I started to read *Fanny Hill*, it was overwhelming and too advanced for me. While reading it, I began to experience the same excitement I felt when Shelton caressed, fondled and sucked my nipples. Not realizing that those feelings were natural, I felt awkward and guilty. It seemed as though I was doing something wrong, so I stopped reading it and decided to have a talk with Ma.

Much to my surprise, Ma welcomed the conversation. She talked about carrying myself like a lady, demanding respect and not allowing men to just use my body. She told me that men will be attracted to me but I should save myself for my husband and not have sex before marriage. Then she told me about the mistakes she made and did not want her children to make the same mistakes and end up like her. Although I always respected Ma, that conversation enabled me to gain a new respect for her. Ma assured me that she was there for me, but, in spite of everything she said, she still didn't tell me that she loved me.

Every Heart Knows Its Own Sorrow

For as long as I could remember, neither of my parents ever told me they loved me. I knew they did, but I needed to hear them tell me that they did. Although Ma was always there and we all knew that she loved us because she took excellent care of us, often depriving herself to make sure we got the things we needed, that was not enough. Children need to be held and told that they are loved. That's why Shelton was so important to me. He told me that he loved me. That's also why so many of those young women we knew fell prey to the pimps who told them they loved them, but really didn't. Everyone needs to feel loved and appreciated and everyone should, first, get that from their parents. That allows them to feel secure and not desperate to obtain that love from others.

So, I was deprived and entered my relationship with Shelton as a deprived, gullible young lady seeking love and attention. Strangely enough, Shelton was in the same boat. I believe that's why we fell so desperately in love with each other. He too never was told, by his parents, that they loved him. Much like Vanessa, he could not wait to leave his father's house. He explained how abusive his father was to his mother and felt like really hurting him, every time he saw his father hurt his mother. Much of the abuse was emotional. His father had another set of children that he fathered while he was married to Shelton's mother. He would bring the other children to the house and expect Shelton's mother to take care of them as though they were her own. Although all of the children got along well with each other, Shelton understood the emotional strain his mother was experiencing.

We both felt like outsiders, misunderstood, and would spend hours talking about our situations and consoling each other. Our commonalities brought us closer together. I received total unconditional love from Shelton. He accepted me as I was. He listened to my wild schemes and was totally engrossed in me, but sex presented a problem for us. I was not going to engage in intercourse. I did not mind kissing and intense petting, but I refused to go all the way. He tried every tactic he could imagine to try to get me to relent but to no avail. Ma said, no sex before marriage and that was that. My abstaining from sexual intercourse with him became quite a problem for us. Several times we severed our relationship for months at a time because of it. I would get tired of tussling with him, trying to fight him off. Moreover, he was exceedingly jealous and would get angry if guys looked at me. I was flirtatious and enjoyed the attention that other guys gave me. I also liked seeing Shelton jealous. That behavior went on for years.

When I graduated from high school, Shelton started talking about getting married, but I wasn't ready for that. I wanted to go to Law school, work, and save some money before getting married. I loved him and there was no doubt in my mind that I wanted to someday marry him, but I also wanted to experience some of the finer things in life before settling down. We also needed to become more in tune with our individual and joint goals. Shelton was naturally gifted in electronics. Whenever there were electrical problems in the apartment building, the super always called Shelton to make the repairs. He majored in that field in high school and I continuously tried to encourage him to pursue it in college. Shelton did not feel that he was college material and refused to try, in spite of my offering to help him. Instead, he accepted a menial job in a factory and seemed content with that and doing electrical repairs on the side. I thought that when he saw how serious I was about pursuing my goals, he would decide to further his education also. However, he never did. Instead, he tried to discourage me from continuing in college.

One day, he went up to City College and saw me with my college counselor. We were in the process of concluding a counseling session. As a SEEK counselor, he was available to assist me with choosing appropriate classes, applying for financial aid and other concerns I might have. It wasn't until Shelton started acting jealous and asking all kinds of questions about my counselor that I took a good look at him and saw him in a different light. Sure enough, my counselor was fine. I had never really paid him any attention until Shelton started asking those questions. Then I noticed that my counselor seemed to have a crush on me. He often needed to see me in his office for things, I felt, he could have handled without me. I also started finding myself becoming more interested in him and Shelton became even more suspicious of our relationship.

On my twentieth birthday Shelton proposed to me. The family had gotten together to celebrate my birthday and I suppose Ma knew about the impending proposal. Shelton's parents and some of our friends were there. For the past year

Shelton had become more persistent about getting married. I suppose he was getting pretty tired of all that petting with no intercourse. I, however, was just fine with our arrangement, but I did notice that Shelton was spending more time supposedly with his friends. He even started going to Baltimore on weekends with his cousin, who was known to be quite a womanizer. We had not resolved the issues around our personal goals, nor had he made any attempts to further his education. When he popped the question and presented me with a ring, about which I had expressed an interest while window shopping one day, I was quite surprised. Of course, I accepted his proposal but did not set a definite wedding date. I still wanted to at least finish college.

Once engaged, Shelton became more aggressive sexually. He demanded that we have sexual intercourse, and one evening, tricked me into going up to his house when his parents were out of town. He made sexual advances and we tussled, but he was persistent. I tried everything to discourage him from forcing himself on me. I told him that I would leave him if he continued to behave in that manner, but he was not listening. I fought with every ounce of strength to ward off his advances, but to no avail. Although I did not feel it, he must have had some penetration because I became pregnant that night.

When I was late getting my period, the next month, I consulted a friend of mine who was in nursing school. She suggested that I wait another week and if it didn't come then I should go to a doctor. Well it did not come and I did go to the doctor. My fears were confirmed. I was pregnant. Shelton was elated when I told him. He immediately started talking about a wedding date but I could not concentrate on a wedding, instead my concentration was on how to tell Ma. I feared telling Ma so much that I toyed with the idea of getting an abortion. Of course, I did not tell Shelton my thoughts. After agonizing about the situation for about another month, I told Ma. She responded by saying "okay, well you two will just have to get married sooner than you planned." Ma was back in the business of planning another wedding. In my heart I knew I wasn't ready to get married, even though I wanted to continue to see Shelton. I knew that he would not understand my dilemma and neither did Ma. I tried to explain it to her but she called it foolishness and insisted that I was getting married.

Life was getting extremely complicated. Even more than ever, I felt; alone, misunderstood and isolated. My dreams and aspirations were fading away and there was no one I could talk to about my feelings. I tried explaining my feelings to Rosetta, but she felt I was just a confused, fickled puppy. She pointed out to me that Shelton and I had been off and on for so many years that if I did not marry him, I would just end up regretting it later. She felt that I was just upset and would get over it when I cooled off a bit. I had no one to turn to. No one understood. I went up to Grandma's house to receive some pampering and to have some private time to think. Grandma never was the type of person to pry into anyone's life, although intuitively she knew when something was wrong. Instead of asking questions, she would just go about her normal tasks of cooking, cleaning and catering to us. Well, when I went to Grandma, she treated me with extra loving care, even allowing me to sleep in her bed. I felt special because no one was allowed to sleep in her bed. Grandma's demeanor communicated to me that she knew what I was going through and it was alright. I finally relented and told Grandma my dilemma. She listened intently, without interrupting me. Usually Grandma was the one who always did the talking, telling us stories. I never knew that she was so understanding. When I finished and broke down in tears, she handed me a tissue and said "Every Heart Knows Its Own Sorrow." She did not say anything else to me but proceeded to call Ma and told her that she needs to leave me alone and not force me to get married. She said that I was not the first girl to get pregnant without being married and I won't be the last. I don't know what Ma said to her, but I was just elated to know that Grandma understood. I had taken a chance of sharing my confusion and fears with Grandma, and she understood. From that day on I felt closer to Grandma then I ever felt before. When I left Grandma's house, I knew everything was going to be fine, regardless of whether I got married or not.

Well, I got married to Shelton. He was very happy saying the vows to me. I, on the other hand, was so nervous that I did not know what was happening. Everything just seemed to be happening so quickly. I was on automatic. Rosetta did an excellent job as my maid of honor, guiding me through the events of the day. I remember, after the wedding ceremony, when we were outside greeting people and taking pictures, my counselor came over to me and gave me a lust filled kiss on my lips. It was clearly not the type of kiss that one would give a bride. It staggered me. Although shocked at the kiss, I rather enjoyed it and thought it should have happened before the wedding, because if it did, maybe there would have been no wedding. Well, Shelton saw the kiss and became very upset. When in the limousine, Shelton referred to the kiss and questioned whether we had kissed like that before. Although I told him that we had never kissed before, he did not believe me. His jealousy would not allow himself to believe me. Of course that detracted from our wedding festivities and the happiness we were suppose to be experiencing. We hardly spoke to each other for the rest of the evening.

Everything was just a blur of, what appeared to be, confusion, except Grandma's reaction to me after the wedding. Grandma never attended any of our weddings because when she attended her first granddaughter's wedding, she performed as though it was a funeral. Everyone in the church was in tears, so it was agreed that she would not attend anymore wedding ceremonies. As I ascended the steps to the reception hall, Grandma was waiting at the top of the steps. When I reached the top step, she grabbed me in a bear hug and wept. It was as though she was weeping for all of the hard times she experienced in the past. She wept for all of the disappointments, loneliness, and heartaches she experienced. She prayed that our union would last forever.

After the reception, we attended the parties that followed at both Ma's house and his parents' house. I was not in a hurry to go home. I was scared to death, because I knew I had to finally have sex with him. He could not wait to get me home to make love, as much as he wanted. Although I was pregnant, in my mind I had not really experienced intercourse, because of the circumstances by which I had become pregnant. Therefore, I felt as though I was still a virgin. Finally, I had to go home. I ran out of places to go and things to do. Shelton kept giving me that knowing look as if saying, I know what you're doing but you have to come home sometime. When we got home I continued to stall for time. I went into the bath tub and stayed in there for about thirty minutes, then he came in. He was totally nude. I had never seen him in the nude before. His body looked firm and strong. His demeanor was calm and knowing. He got into the tub with me, which I thought was nasty. How could he get into the same bath water. That was unsanitary. I had the nerve to say that to him and he just started laughing. Then he decided to get playful by splashing water on me. Some water got in my hair and all hell broke loose. I started yelling, how could he wet my hair? I did not have a straightening comb at the house. We had to go over to Ma's house the next day and everyone would know what we had been doing. By this time Shelton was dying with laughter. He knew I was naive, but had no idea that I was as naive as I was. After laughing a hearty laugh, which only served to enrage me even more, he took me in his arms and gently made sweet love to me over and over again.

BETRAYED

Our marital bliss lasted two months, then the arguments began. He felt I was a mama's girl, since I still maintained close ties to Ma. I had not really accepted being a married woman and all of the responsibilities that went along with that. For instance, I wanted Shelton and I to visit Ma's house every day, but he was not receptive to that. He wanted us to be alone together in our apartment as much as possible, but I was not accustomed to that and did not see the need for us to spend so much time alone together. Being brought up in a large family, I was accustomed to having a lot of people around all of the time. I needed time to gradually adjust to being alone with Shelton, but we did not know how, probably because of our immaturity, to resolve that problem in a reasonable manner. Instead we argued without listening to each other's rationale. I felt he was being unreasonable and selfish and he thought I was a big mama's girl. We had not developed a way to listen to each other in a respectful understanding manner. Had we known how to work through our problems, life would have been happier for both of us because we truly loved each other. Moreover, we did not have anyone to talk to about our marital problems. Our parents were not good role models. They made a mess of their own marriages, so we knew they could not give us guidance in ours. Every married couple we knew were experiencing their own problems and were not doing a good job resolving them. The idea of seeking professional help did not occur to us because we had never been exposed to the idea of going to professional counselors for help. That was just not done. Ma did not encourage me to stay home because she enjoyed having her children around and did not see my visiting every day as a problem either. Nicole had been doing the same thing, so ma's thinking was, if she did it then it must be all right. Little did I know, Nicole's husband was complaining about the same thing.

My complaint about Shelton was that I thought he needed to make more money and be more considerate and helpful, since I was pregnant and very often did not feel like cooking. Although most evenings he would meet me at Ma's house after work, he did not want to eat at Ma's house. Instead, he expected me to prepare a hot meal at our house every night, but there were times when I did not feel up to cooking. Shelton was not understanding of my feelings and insisted that I prepare his meals each day.

As my pregnancy progressed, cooking became less of a priority for me. I insisted that we continue to meet at Ma's house where we starting eating dinner almost every evening. He began to resent going to Ma's house and I began to resent the fact that he was not making enough money to support us. I began to worry about how we were going to survive financially when I had to stop working my part-time job. My pregnancy was progressing and each day I felt the discomfort of it. I knew that I would either have to stop working or stop going to school and I was determined to finish school. Whenever I attempted to discuss our financial situation with Shelton, he would dismiss me with a shrug. We needed to start making plans for the baby, but he refused to discuss anything about money. Out of total frustration, I would start cursing which would them result in both of us screaming at each other and nothing would be resolved. Soon, our communication became even more hostile; calling each other names and pointing out each others' weaknesses. There were many nights when I slept on the couch because I did not want to be in the same room with him and he refused to get out of the bed. Married life was no fun. We were falling out of love and did not know how to salvage it. I was not happy and did not know how to communicate my unhappiness to my husband without cursing and being disrespectful. He was probably feeling the same way. We were two young people starting a family and had no idea how to handle it. We were sinking fast without a life line. I found myself dreading going home. We hardly talked to each other. The wonderful times and open communication we experienced, most of the time, during our four years of courtship had disappeared. We were no longer friends and I missed our friendship. I found myself crying a lot because I did not want our marriage to be that way, but unable to express my feelings to Shelton, I held them in and sank into despair. It quickly got to the point where we were only going through the motions of being a married couple.

Then the unthinkable happened. One of his friends called to speak with Shelton. After finding out that Shelton was not at home, he proceeded to hold a conversation with me. It was not unusual for me to have conversations with Shelton's friends because we all used to hang out together. Moreover, that particular friend had a crush on me. Actually, I met him at the same time I met Shelton. He was also at my cousin's wedding and had arrived with Shelton. He made advances toward me at the wedding, but Shelton was the only one of interest to me. Throughout our courtship, this particular friend always told me what was going on with Shelton when I was not around. Shelton knew the guy liked me but never worried because he knew I was not interested.

During the conversation, he told me that Shelton had a child . The child was born two weeks before our wedding and the mother had attended the wedding, without my knowledge. She was Shelton sister's friend, with whom I was not acquainted. The information was devastating to me. Without saying another word, I hung up the telephone. I felt like my world had ended. The other problems we had were nothing in comparison to this. This problem could not go away, even with counseling. He had gotten another female pregnant while we were seeing each other. He had a child and did not share that information with me. How could I ever trust him again? There was an empty, hollow void in my spirit. I felt betrayed.

When Shelton came home, before I could ask him about the information I had just learned, he demanded to be fed. Determined to be calm about the baby situation so I could hear his side of the story, I calmly told him that there was a tuna platter in the refrigerator and crackers in the cupboard. After taking the tuna platter out of the refrigerator, he came into the room and threw it on the floor and said, "this is rabbit food." That was the straw that broke the camel's back. I was furious and told him that he could take the food and shove it up his ass. Then I told him what I had learned about his child. He was dumbfounded and began to ask me how I found out. With that confirmation, I told him he could kiss my ass.

Now I was really cursing, using the curse words I heard while growing up in Harlem. While growing up, my parents never allowed us to curse. We did not even say the word liar. Instead we would say storyteller. I was angry at myself for allowing this cheating pig to make me sin my soul. These thoughts were racing through my mind while I was packing my clothes. He begged me not to go and tried to explain to me how it happened. He tried to blame it on me because while we were going together I refused to have sex. He then started seeing another young lady who was willing to have sex with him. He pleaded with me not to go and expressed his undying love for me. I would not hear it. All I knew was that while he was trying to persuade me to marry him, he had been having sex with someone else. I lost respect for him. How could he have her at our wedding? How could he plan on marrying me and not tell me that he had a child? Was he planning to do to me what his father did to his mother? As I asked him those questions, I saw a change come over him. Now he was angry. I had equated him to his father, the person he loathed. As I continued to point out his similarities to his father, he became outraged and landed a smashing blow to my left jaw. When the blow landed, I struggled to maintain my balance but fell to the floor. He got on top of me and continued to hit me, as though he was out of his mind. Then, as if coming to his senses, he started kissing me all over and apologizing for hitting me. I tried pushing him off of me but he was too strong and I was weakened by the blows. While crying, I was asking myself, was this really happening or was it a bad dream? I could not believe that Shelton had hit me. How could he? How could he profess loving me and be able to strike me, especially in my condition? There was absolutely no excuse for becoming physically abusive. I had witnessed the result of my mother's experience of being hit by Daddy and I was not going to chance hanging around with Shelton to receive the same kind of abusive treatment again. This was the end of our love affair. I remembered what Grandma taught us about apologies and said to him, if you didn't mean to hit me then you would not have hit me. I was not accepting his apology, to hell with him. I could be miserable by myself. I did not need all of that aggravation. Crying uncontrollably, I called Ma and told her to come get me. Within an hour Ma, Richie, Gregory and Kevin were at the door. Without saying a word to me, Richie went into the bedroom where Shelton was laying down. He closed the door. I was happy that

Richie was going to kick his ass but I didn't hear any noise. He was not getting his ass kicked. Why wasn't Richie kicking his ass? He deserved it. If I thought I could, I would have kicked his ass my damn self. After about five minutes, Richie came out of the room and said to me and my family, "come on let's go." I was disappointed that Richie did not inflict bodily harm on Shelton, but I dared not mention that to Richie. So, we took my things to Ma's house and I never went back to Shelton, in spite of his numerous attempts to get me to come back.

Two months after I left Shelton, I delivered a beautiful baby girl. She was a beautiful cocoa brown, like her father and a head full of hair, like me. She was my pride and joy. All of my energy went into caring and providing for my Karen. The sun, moon and stars shone on her; nothing else in the world was as important to me. Although I continued in school, I worked after school to support us. Ma was a great support. While I worked and attended school, she took care of Karen. I did not have to worry about whether she was receiving proper care. As she grew, people thought she was Rosetta's child because she looked more like Rosetta than me. Rosetta was also a great support. She also worked and helped to provide financial support for Karen. She was flattered that Karen looked like her and would buy something nice for her each payday. She was like a second mother to her and I knew that I could depend on her for support and friendship. Although I no longer had a husband, I was provided with loving people to give me the support I needed.

Shelton had stopped calling and I heard that he started

living with the woman and his child. At weak moments I thought about the good times that Shelton and I shared throughout the years and would start to cry. In my lonely bed, late at night when everyone else was asleep, I would sob and ache for Shelton's loving arms and yearned to hear his strong voice telling me how much he loved me. I remembered when we first met and how he enchanted me. Our love had been a dream come true. Then things had changed. They had spun out of control and we did not know how to fall back in love again. During those lonely nights, I would look at Karen while she slept and cry because she was not going to experience her father's love. Cry because he was not there to cradle her in his arms and whisper in her ears "Daddy loves you." She would never experience the moments of joy that I shared with my father. She would never know how it felt to lay on her father's shoulders and watch him read, the way I did with Daddy. She would not experience the joy of her father building a chicken coop for her chickens with his own hands. I cried for all of us.

When I needed a man to talk to, I would hang out with Karen's Godfather, Lloyd, a long time friend that I grew up with on 7th Avenue. He provided me with an understanding ear. We hung out together, mostly meeting after work and going to pubs tasting different types of imported draft beers and eating corned beef sandwiches. We considered ourselves connoisseurs of imported beers but the real deal was, we liked the high we got from drinking strongly brewed beer. Occasionally, we would go to Lloyd's apartment where he would prepare exquisite meals. He was known for his gourmet dishes which I totally enjoyed. It was always a pleasure hanging out with him and we would share stories about our love lives. He had recently divorced and was feeling alone and misunderstood, just like me. Our relationship helped me to realize that men also experience the same type of heartache and pain, from failed love relationships. I always thought that men were unfeeling whenever their relationships ended. Love them, leave them and move on to the next victim is what I envisioned as men's attitudes. Our platonic relationship was enlightening because I was also able to reciprocate in helping Lloyd to understand how women felt in certain situations. Our friendship grew and I knew that Karen and I could always depend on him if the going got rough. When we lived in Harlem, our families were close and often got together at parties. Lloyd always had a crush on Rosetta, but she did not feel the same way towards him and he never pushed the issue. As the years progressed, we continued to be there for each other for spiritual support. It was always refreshing to be with a man who was supportive, understanding and kind. He was like a brother to me.

CONFUSION

I can personally attest to the verity of the adage "into each life some tears must fall." Tears became part of my everyday life. Although I went about my life, doing the things I had to do to survive, I was not happy and felt empty inside. The only joy I felt was seeing Karen's smiling face when I entered the room, cradling her in my arms and knowing she was mine to love as much as I wanted. There wasn't anything I wouldn't do for her. It seemed every time I laid my eyes on her, I could not get enough of her. I felt that she was all I had in my life that made me happy and the only one who gave me unconditional love. She loved me in spite of my shortcomings. I did not have to change my ways because she loved me for me and I loved her with all my heart. One day when Grandma came to visit us, she sat silently on the couch and watched the interaction between me and Karen. Then, she called me over to her and in the manner that she always communicated, said "God is a jealous God and if you put anyone above him, he will snatch them away." She said no more. That shook me to my very soul. From that day on I was careful not to place Karen above God. But I did not stop displaying my love for her and telling her so. However, I remembered to thank God for blessing me with the privilege of having the responsibility of raising that wonderful gift from God. As the years passed, I began to better understand that it pleased God that I cherished his gift to me and instead of being jealous, he was pleased, because he knew my heart.

Grandma passed away one year later. It devastated the entire family. She was the link that held us together. We always knew that Grandma was there for us all. She provided comfort and protection, not only for us, but for anyone who knew her. She embodied unselfishness and often made huge sacrifices to help others. In fact, she died as a result of helping someone else. While taking an elderly friend of hers to a clinic appointment, Grandma, who was also elderly, slipped and fell. As a result, she suffered internal bleeding and never recovered from her injuries. Among the many fond memories I have of her, her many words of wisdom often ring in my ears. Although Grandma is no longer living, in the flesh, her kind, loving, wise spirit lives on and I thank God that I was blessed with having Grandma in my life.

To fill the empty void I felt inside, I decided to experience the world and have fun. While in graduate school, I met two women who were also divorced with children and several years older than me. Bunchie, was the most recently divorced and had been married the longest out of the three of us. Aside from her recent divorce, she had also experienced the loss of her brother, who was her only sibling. When we met, she too was depressed and feeling alone. Her mother had passed away some years earlier and she only had her father, her children and some other relatives who she could depend on for reassurance and support. We quickly developed a friendship and gradually started relating to each other as sisters. We both were relatively naive and had very little experience with the singles scene. We have been there, through the years, trying to help each other muddle through the maze of failed relationships. Unlike with Rosetta, who has always had very little patience with me regarding matters of the heart, I have been able to share those confused experiences with Bunchie. However, neither of us were any good at figuring out what we were doing wrong. My other friend, unlike Bunchie and I, had been divorced for several years and had jumped right into the singles scene with no hesitation. She was very promiscuous and knowledgeable about men. Since I was still very naive about men, I found myself intrigued with her accounts of her sexual escapades. She told me about her sexual encounters and other experiences with men. She went to great lengths to please her numerous sexual partners. She talked about having oral sex as though it was a totally natural thing. I had no idea that people put penises in their mouths and was shocked when she told me that men "went down" on her. Moreover, she liked it. How could they do those things? It made me think twice about kissing men. As a result of hearing her stories, I decided whenever I go out with men I would not kiss them on the first date and then not until we have talked about their sexual preferences. I decided that if a man admitted to going down on women then I would have nothing to do with him because his mouth must be full of germs. Now, I was totally confused. I thought Shelton and I had complete sexual experiences. At no time had he mentioned wanting to go down on me and he never asked me to suck his penis. I don't know what I would have done if he would have asked me. I began to wonder about what else I did not know about sex. This sex thing was becoming more and more complicated. My friend was totally uninhibited. She told me of many one night stands where she took men to her house, engaged in oral and anal sex and then never saw the guys again. Moreover, they did not use condoms, especially since Aids was not yet a known virus. I was somewhat intrigued with her carefree life-style but could not venture into quite the extremes that she did. Since she told me that I have not lived until someone goes down on me, I became curious and wanted to try it.

My chance came when I met an absolutely overwhelmingly, handsome man at one of my friend's parties. He was my age, six feet two inches tall and weighed about 190 pounds. He had broad shoulders, a wide pleasing smile, brown skin and his hair was in a full Afro. I was sitting with Rosetta at a table at a then popular night club called Small's Paradise. I had not noticed him two tables ahead of me until he turned around, smiled at me and very slowly started licking his lips in a very sensual manner. At first I glanced away, somewhat embarrassed, but then could not help looking back at him. In a knowing way, he looked me straight in my eyes and blew me a kiss and licked his lips again. I was totally intrigued with him and knew that he would probably be my first one night stand. When the DJ started playing *Billy Jean*, the lip licker came over to me, asked me to dance, took my hand before I could answer and lead me onto the dance floor. Although the song had a fast tempo, he took me in his arms, held me close to him forcing my body to sway with his sensual movements. I noticed that he was very strong and smelled delicious. He literally swept me off my feet. Before I knew it, he was cradling me in his arms and carrying me off the dance floor and into the lobby of the dance hall. Then, he started kissing me with an overwhelming urgency that I could not ignore. He dominated me and I felt helpless. He continued to kiss me until I totally submitted and kissed him back with a hunger that surprised me. It had been a long time since I felt such passion, and I wanted to savor every moment. While we continued to kiss, he continued to cradle me in his arms. I remember thinking that this guys is damn strong to be able to hold me all this time. Although I was thin, I still weighed about 160 pounds and was five feet eleven inches tall. Reluctantly, we stopped kissing when some people came into the lobby and wanted to exit, but we were blocking the doorway. He put me down and introduced himself as Dean. I introduced myself and, in a flirtatious manner, asked him whether that was the way he introduced himself to all women. He responded by saying, "only you." Although I knew it was just a line, I liked it. If Rosetta had not been with me, I know I would have gone home with him that night. Just looking at him excited me.

I was totally attracted to him sexually. We went back and joined the party and danced almost every dance together. During the slow jams, he held me tightly in his strong muscular arms and our bodies swayed in a slow rhythmic motion eager to experience more. When it was time to go, he asked me if I would go home with him. With all my heart I wanted to say yes, but I told him that I do not go home with men I just meet at parties. He looked into my eyes and said, "you know that you want to go home with me. Let's not play silly games with each other. It's rare that two people are so attracted to each other. I want to taste you and I know you feel the same about me." As he spoke, I felt my legs giving out. I was getting physically weak. I wanted that man so badly I could taste it, and he knew it too. But I told him that we would have to hook up some other time because I came with my sister and we always leave together. I gave him my telephone number and suggested that he call me sometime. He walked me and Rosetta to my car, gave me a soft kiss on my cheek, assured me that he would call and walked away. As I was sharing my excitement with Rosetta, he pulled up next to us, honked his horn, blew me a kiss and sped away in his dark green Jaguar. Rosetta and I could not believe our eyes. Mr. lip licker, Dean, was not only handsome, strong and sexy but also had a baaad ride. I felt like I hit the jackpot. I was going to experience great sex with a gorgeous man and ride in a luxury car. What more could a girl want? Little did I know then that I would want something from him that he could not or would not give.

Just as I entered the apartment, the telephone started

ringing. I rushed in and somewhat out of breath, picked up the phone. The voice on the other line said that he liked the panting sounds that I was making and wanted to come and get me right away. Pleased that he was anxious to see me, since he obviously could not wait to call, I responded by saying that I could pant louder and heavier, given the right stimuli. Unshaken by my banter, he said, "then give me your address and I'll be right over." He was obviously not a pushover who I could tease. He was not backing down. It was as though he could read my mind and knew that I wanted him as much as he wanted me. Our intense energy and desire for each other could be felt through the telephone. For the first time in my life, I was at a loss for words. He was in control and we both knew it and I liked it. There was no doubt in my mind that we were going to have great sex. Somehow I managed to persuade him to take me out to lunch on Monday, then we could talk more about what we wanted to do. Reluctantly he agreed but stated that the only reason why he was going along with that plan was because he did not have my address. He said that if he did, he would be at my door in twenty minutes. When we hung up, my heart was racing. He aroused me to the point of exhaustion, and that was just from talking to him. Imagine what it was going to be like actually making love with him. I could not sleep, the anticipation was overwhelming. I kept fantasizing about how we were going to make love, but I knew that because of my limited experience, my fantasies were limited as well. There was no way that I could have imagined how wonderful it actually was.

Every Heart Knows Its Own Sorrow

On Monday morning I woke up earlier than usual so I would have enough time to carefully choose my attire. Everything had to be just right. I wanted to look sexy but in a subtle way, without seeming obvious. I selected a cotton dress that appeared, at first glance, to be a prairie dress that was popular then, but upon further examination was very sexy. It was deep blue with cuffed long sleeves and very small cranberry colored flowers throughout the pattern of the dress. The top of the dress, from the neck to the waist, was form fitting with small delicate dark blue buttons that were unfastened to my bust, revealing some cleavage but not a lot. It revealed just enough to make a man want to see more. The waistline of the dress arched up on the sides to just above my waist and then the front and back of the waist peaked downward, then connected to the loosely draped skirt of the dress, which flowed just below my knees. I wore cranberry colored opened toe heels, with silky sheer off black panty hose and black lace panties and bra.

I could not concentrate in class in anticipation of what was to come. He arrived at the school promptly at noon. I was just walking toward the door when I saw him open the door, looking around to make sure that he was at the right place. He was wearing a gray sports jacket, a black cotton shirt that was unbuttoned to the chest revealing soft curly hair, black pants and black shoes. In his left hand he was carrying one long stem rose. I called to him and he smiled. As I approached him, taking long graceful strides, his smile became more pronounced as he started licking his lips. In my mind I was saying, "just keep on licking those lips, soon I'm going to give you something else to lick." He then started walking toward me and as we met, we embraced and kissed a long, lustful kiss. He took my right hand and gently placed the rose in it without saying a word. I smiled, said thank you and gave him a soft kiss on his cheek. We then left and walked to his Jaguar that was parked in front of the building. As I was getting into the car, I hoped my friends were watching. I wanted them to see the gorgeous specimen I was with and wishfully gaze upon that beautiful Jaguar.

We went to a cute diner in Queens. We both ordered sandwiches, but neither of us really wanted to eat food. However, as we nibbled at our food, we made small talk about school, our jobs and families. He told me that he was single and worked as a fireman. That accounted for his ability to pick me up the way he did at the party. I became even more excited as I fantasized being picked up and carried by him again, this time as a prelude to delicious, exciting love making. Distracted by my fantasies, I tried focusing on what he was saying about actively pursuing a Bachelor's degree at John Jay College. When I told him that Rosetta taught at John Jay, he said that he did hear about her through some friends who had taken her course. We realized that we had a lot in common. He also grew up in Harlem and was familiar with its milieu, but moved to Queens, as a teenager, since drugs had become rampant in the projects where he lived. He attended the same Junior High School as Rosetta, in the Bronx, but had not known her there. We talked a little more about ourselves, then he asked, "so what do you want to do?" I responded by asking him what he wanted to do? Without hesitating, he said, "I want to do the same thing I wanted to do to you the other night, take you home and make love to you." I had not anticipated such directness; it caught me by surprise and I started to blush. Then he said, "come on let's go." He got up, paid the bill and whisked me off into his car.

As he drove, he periodically glanced over at me. We did not speak. I did not know what to say, so I stared out of the window but at nothing in particular. I was nervous and had no idea about how to act or what to say. This was the first time that I was going to make love to someone other than Shelton. I began to wonder whether he would laugh at my inexperience? Should I back out and ask him to drive me home? I decided to go through with it especially since I was so attracted to him. Besides it was bound to happen sometime, so why not now? As we approached a high-rise apartment building, he turned to me and said, "this is where I live." Then he pulled into the building's parking garage, parked in his spot, turned off the ignition, placed his hand on my thigh and asked if I was ok. Hoarsely, I responded that I was fine and managed a slight smile. He then got out of the car and opened the door for me. Taking my hand, he gently helped me out of the car, took me in his arms and gave me a gentle kiss. It was as though he knew that I had never done this before and was doing all the right things to help me relax. I appreciated his compassion, which was a big turn on for me. I felt myself relaxing and tuning into him. As we took the elevator up to his apartment, I held my head down and looked at the floor, avoiding eye contact with him.

Gently, he lifted my chin, kissed me on my forehead and when the elevator door opened, lead me to his apartment. I had not anticipated his apartment to look like it did. It was a large one room studio apartment. It was sparsely furnished with a brown imitation fur couch, a lamp table and lamp, a kitchen table with a typewriter and books piled on it and two kitchen chairs, and exercise equipment. There was also a wall unit that had a record player, TV, a few wooden statues, and pictures of him in uniform. The apartment looked like it needed to be cleaned. Obviously, that was not his forte.

When he finished locking the door, he came over to me and we kissed. At first, I was uncomfortable and nervous, but as he held me and I felt his strong arms and eager body caressing me, I could not help but surrender. His kisses were hot and strong. His tongue thrashed about my mouth as if searching desperately for mine. As I embraced his tongue with mine, I felt the warm sweet excitement envelop my being. Our bodies throbbed and ached to feel the depths of each other. We raced to undress each other as though we had an uncontrollable urge that had to be satisfied immediately. He pulled out the bed from his convertible couch and laid me on it, gently parting my thighs and revealing the lush jet black hair that concealed my most private possession. He placed his warm hand there and began stroking the cavity of my being. My body eagerly arched itself toward him begging for more. Then he took both of my breasts in his hands and started licking and sucking each nipple until my body shook with excitement. He gradually started kissing and caressing my stomach, and

119

navel. Then his tongue ventured through my forest and found my most sensitive area. He continued his licking and sucking until my body shook and exploded with ecstasy. I cried out his name and he then mounted me and with confident, strong thrusts, penetrated my being and continued until he cried out some inaudible words and exploded in me. Totally exhausted, we laid next to each other, barely touching trying to cool our bodies. As I laid there, I thought about what my friend had told me and she was right. I truly had not lived until he had gone down on me. And I wanted more.

We spent the rest of the day making love together and each time, he exposed me to something new and exciting. His energy was boundless and I was grateful. After our love making, he drove me home, walked me to my door, gave me a kiss and promised to call. Days passed and I did not hear from him. I listened to news reports to find out whether there were any serious fires that might have involved him. My upbringing did not allow me to call him. He was the man and should call me first. I agonized and ached for him. How could he not call me? I began to think that maybe it was not as good to him as it was to me, because if it was, there was no way that he would not call me. Was this what one night stands felt like? I did not like it. Was I not suppose to think about him anymore? Maybe I just didn't know how to play the game, so I called my friends and told them everything. Bunchie was intrigued with the story, but could not offer any helpful advice regarding my dilemma. My other friend however, was chock full of advice. First, she congratulated me on getting my first head job, then she told me that if I wanted to see him again, then I should call him. She explained that I needed to get rid of those old fashioned ideas about not calling the man. If I wanted to see him, then I should just call him and not wonder about whether he felt the same about me. She reminded me that I was not involved with him to get married, but that I liked the way he made love to me, so I should ask for more. That thinking was totally foreign to me and it meant that I would have to swallow my pride and call him. There was something in my being that warned me against calling him. Was I willing to sacrifice my pride for lust? Then what would he think of me? I never wanted anyone to think of me as being a common woman. I thought about all those things and decided that if he did not think enough of me to call, then I would not compromise myself and call him. I needed, at least, his respect.

He finally called me after two weeks and explained that the reason why he had not called sooner was because his girlfriend had a baby girl the day after we had made love. I was flabbergasted. I knew he was single but had not thought to ask him whether he had a girlfriend or children. He was very nonchalant about our encounter and did not seem to think it unusual that he did not bother to call me during the two weeks. This was a first for me, because Shelton had always kept in touch with me while we were dating. I did not know what to do. On one hand I wanted to tell him off. How dare he have the audacity not to call me? Then, on the other hand, I desperately wanted to see him again. If I got high and mighty with him and told him off, I would be taking a chance of not seeing him again. Not willing to risk that, I told him that I had been worried about him and thought that something terrible had happened to him. I suggested that, in the future, I would appreciate it if he would give me a quick call to allay my fears. His response was, "I can respect that."

He ended up not being a one night stand, however our relationship, through the years, resembled a series of one night stands. We would meet from time to time explicitly to have blissful sex and then not speak to each other for weeks or months at a time as he continued his relationship with his girlfriend and I entered into empty relationships with other men. Although I had very strong feelings for him, I knew that our relationship could not proceed in the direction I would have liked. If he had not already been involved with someone else, I could have allowed myself to fall in love with him. Not only did we have wonderful sex together, but we could also talk to each other, sharing our innermost desires. However, he was dedicated to his girlfriend and child and I knew that his feelings for me were not stronger than his feelings for them. Moreover, I respected him for giving them the time and devotion that he did. I felt that he was a manly man, willing and able to take on his responsibilities. As time went on, we became friends and I began to rely on seeing him whenever one of my other relationships failed. It seemed he knew when I needed to see him because he always called at the right time. We eventually reached a point where we did not have to have sex but would talk for hours about situations occurring in our lives. I was searching for the same feeling I felt with Shelton, before we had gotten married. I wanted to be loved and in love, but Dean and everyone else I met could not fill that void. I no longer laughed from the depth of my soul. My laughter was now superficial and meaningless. One of my friends said to me, "don't let them take your smile away," but it was already fading. That bright, loquacious, gregarious young lady was becoming withdrawn and insecure. I felt trapped in a tightly sealed box, with no escape. No one was hearing my cries for help.

Without realizing it, I was attracting the same types of people to me; losers. I was feeling like a loser and losers attract losers. I was compromising my dignity and self-worth, and was settling for scraps. It seemed as though men sensed my despair and those not feeling sorry for themselves, did not want to be around me. I was a repellent for men who were upbeat and happy, but I did not realize that I was responsible for that by sending out negative energy. Therefore, I developed relationships with men like Arnold. He was seventeen years older than me and recently separated from his wife. He was a pathetic pot head and alcoholic, who cried whenever he got drunk, but he treated me like a princess. He made me feel safe and protected. I needed him to make me feel special since I did not feel that way about myself. There wasn't anything that he would not do for me. I wished I felt the same about him, but I didn't. He ensured that all of my financial needs were taken care of. He gave me a weekly allowance that assisted with child care and enabled me to purchase some of the things I liked. Everyday he confessed his undying love for me and eventually he became overwhelming. I got sick and tired of his whining and overprotectiveness. Moreover, he did not satisfy me sexually. Although we engaged in oral sex, it was not close to being as enjoyable as with Dean. Soon I found myself thinking of other men when I was with him, and I felt guilty about that. He was so good to me, but it was not enough to make me love him. I began to wonder if I could ever love anyone again. An empty, hollow feeling was my constant companion. As I attempted to search my heart to try to understand my problem, the answers did not come. Perhaps I did not know how to search my heart. Perhaps I did not know my heart. I was so confused and lost, and I did not know what to do or where to turn. When I attended church services, I found myself unable to surrender to that unknown power as so many of the parishioners could. It was as though I could not let myself go. I was afraid to relinquish control of myself to that unknown entity. Yet, was I really in control? At least I thought I was. So I went on feeling alone, depressed and misunderstood.

After two years of being in that depressing and aimless relationship, I told him that I was not happy with him. In reality, I was not happy with myself. I did not know then, that in order to be happy with someone else, you must first be happy with yourself. No one else can make you happy, that's your job. Other people can only supplement your happiness, but happiness begins with self, first. When I told Arnold about how unhappy I was with him, it only made him more of a nuisance. He set out to prove that he could make me love him by spending more money and constantly sending me greeting cards, confessing his undying love for me. The truth of the matter was that he was just as miserable as I was. He was just as lost and confused. There was no way that our relationship could have survived. However, Ma liked him and felt that I would learn to love him. Her logic made no sense to me. Either I loved him or I didn't. What would make me learn to love him? I was not accepting her logic. I believe it's a true saying "God watches over fools and babies," because I was the biggest fool and, come to think of it, a big baby as well. Well, thank God I had the presence of mind not to hold on to that dead end relationship. Although I disliked hurting him, he had to go. Granted, I was depressed, but he just added to the depression.

As I was ending my relationship with Arnold, I met a lawyer. We gradually began to date. He was also recently separated and fourteen years my senior. Even more than Arnold, he provided me with nice things. Until I met him, I had limited exposure to the finer things in life. He exposed me to a world I never knew existed. We traveled to exotic places in the Caribbean where we stayed at exclusive resorts, spent a lot of his money in casinos, skinny-dipped and made wild love wherever and whenever we wanted. We ate at some of the best restaurants in New York and attended Broadway plays. He introduced me to Jazz and the Alvin Ailey Dance Company. We developed a close friendship. I helped him decorate his luxury apartment on the Upper West Side of Manhattan and he helped me find my own apartment, in which Rosetta insisted on coming to live with me. I welcomed her company, because I did not want to live by myself with Karen. Plus, with Rosetta there, he would not feel so comfortable spending the night. I liked him, but I knew that I was not in love with him. It was fun dating him, until I learned that he was seeing someone else. A mutual friend of ours told me about the other woman. I was very angry, especially since I knew the person he was seeing and had a great deal of respect for her. We had attended Columbia University together when I was pursuing my master's degree and she a doctorate. I was not going for that, not from him. He could not pleasure me the way Dean did, so why should I accept him seeing someone else. My feeling was, I did not accept that from my husband, the man I loved, so I was not going to take it from him, a mere passing romance. So I abruptly ended the relationship after I convinced him to send me on an all expense paid vacation to St.Thomas, in the Virgin Islands. I enjoyed myself immensely and when, upon my return, he picked me up at the airport and drove me home, without an explanation, I told him that I did not want to see him any longer. As he pleaded for an explanation, I exited the car and never looked back.

Life was becoming more and more complicated. Alone in my room, I remember crying out "Why are people so deceitful?" I feared that I was also learning how to be deceitful and did not like it. Was this the way of the world? Would I ever find someone honest, loving and true? In my mind, my cries were directed to no one or nothing in particular. All I knew was that I had a strong urge to cry out. Maybe, in my heart, I was hoping that someone would hear me, someone would care. In the fairy tales, Prince Charming always rescued the damsel in distress and they lived happily ever after. Where was my Prince Charming? I wanted happiness ever after and I wanted someone to give it to me. Little did I know, it did not work that way. Fairy tales were unreal. Life was not that simple. There were lessons, trials and tribulation still to come.

As a way of trying to ease the pain and loneliness that I was feeling, I started going to disco clubs and parties. Every weekend there was a party for me to attend. My friends were heavy into the disco scene, so I got involved also. Since I loved to dance, it was not unusual to see me doing the hustle with a number of the very good dancers at the clubs. When I danced, consumed in the music, I forgot about everything and everyone. It became an escape for me. No one could disappoint me while I was dancing. I was carefree and momentarily happy, until the music ended and reality reared its depressing head again. Aside from dancing, I found temporary happiness in the arms of strangers.

Time after time I entered into unhealthy relationships. There was one however, that got me to look at myself, physically, as a beautiful women. Again, he was a much older man. He was so old, he refused to tell me his age. Although he looked good, ate well and was athletic, I knew he was at least twenty years older than me. Why did I find myself with older men? Was I somehow reaching out for my father's love? Or, was I subconsciously putting myself with men I knew were unavailable, to shield myself from commitment? Or, maybe all of the above. Whatever it was, I was sinking deeper and deeper into mass confusion and despair. I was just not learning the lessons I needed to learn, because I kept making the same mistakes over and over again and ending up in unhealthy relationships.

We met in the Bahamas during a vacation I took with Ma and Karen. I had no intentions of meeting or dating any guys while on that trip. All I wanted to do was enjoy the company of my mother and daughter. That was the first vacation the three of us had ever taken together. It was quite special as it allowed me to be with Ma in a different environment. We were having a very nice time, except for the annoying Island men who constantly harassed us as we entered and left the hotel. I was in no mood for dealing with unwelcome advances. Ma seemed to be oblivious to them.

Johnny and I met one day when Ma, Karen and I were sitting in the lobby of the hotel waiting for our tour bus to arrive. A group of approximately thirty newly arrived travelers noisily entered the hotel lobby, obviously very excited to be in the Bahamas. The group consisted mostly of young women and a few men. I had been on the Island for three days and by that time was totally annoyed with the rude advances by the Island men, so I deliberately tried to make myself look unattractive. My hair was braided in two corn rolls, one on each side of my head. I was wearing a t-shirt, a pair of faded cut off denim shorts, sandals and an unwelcome scowl on my face.

Some of the travelers were experiencing difficulty at the registration desk when a rather attractive, stately gentleman approached the registration desk and began negotiating on behalf of the travelers. I later learned, he was the group's organizer. I noticed the confident manner in which he handled the business, which made him attractive to me. When he completed the business and everyone in the group had gone to their rooms, he turned around and looked in my direction and our eyes met. I shyly looked away as he started walking in my direction. Much to my surprise he came over to me and introduced himself. Then he politely turned to Ma, introduced himself and said to Karen, "and who is this lovely young lady." Karen gave him a wide grin displaying her missing front teeth. Ma quickly introduced herself and I reluctantly introduced myself, all the while thinking, "he is one of those jive dudes who thinks he can pull any woman." I was determined not to be one of those women. He said he was glad to meet us and asked whether we were staying at that hotel, where were we from and how long were we going to be staying on the Island? He was wasting no time. He seemed to know that he had won Ma over, since she had a grin on her face from one ear to the other. I, however, was playing it cool. Ma quickly responded to all of his questions. He was happy to hear that we were from New York City and informed us that he lived in Queens, approximately forty minutes away from us. That widened Ma's grin even more. The tour bus came just as he was about to say something to me. Not wanting to get involved in a prolonged conversation, since I was not interested in dealing with any men during that trip, I abruptly got up, extended my hand to him and said, "it was nice meeting you and I hope you enjoy your vacation." I motioned to Ma and Karen to get up. Without hesitating, he asked if I would like to attend a party the group was having that evening. I politely told him that I would probably be too tired after the tour, then thanked him for the invitation. Then we boarded the tour bus. When we were seated, Ma commented on his good looks and said that he reminded her of Daddy. He did resemble Daddy in the manner in which he carried himself. A sharp dresser with a style much like Daddy's, he stood very erect with an air of confidence and a take charge attitude. Ma encouraged me to go to the party, since he seemed like such a nice man. My response to her was "sometimes looks are deceiving." I did find him appealing, especially the way he handled himself. However, I felt an uneasy feeling inside me. He reminded me of those charming pimps that Rosetta and I observed while looking out of our 7th Avenue window.

When we returned from the tour, there was a message for me, at the front desk, from Johnny telling me that the invitation was still open and he would be honored if I came as his guest. He left the telephone number to his room and asked me to call him by 7:00pm to inform him of my decision. Ma, Karen and I took a nap and when we woke up, went to dinner. After dinner, Ma suggested that I go to the party since I had not done any partying thus far, while on the trip. She said that I was a young person and needed to enjoy myself. After considering her words, I decided to attend the party. I called Johnny at 6:45pm and told him I would like to attend the party. He was elated and asked how long it would take for me to get ready. When I told him an hour, he told me that he had to make sure that everything was properly arranged for the party, and would pick me up at eight.

He arrived promptly at eight and was visibly shocked when he saw me. I had combed out my hair into a rather full Afro and was wearing a very low cut form fitting black gown with black and white accessories. The dress revealed my voluptuous size 36DD breasts, which he could not take his eyes off. Obviously in a state of shock, his pipe fell out of his mouth and he had to scramble to retrieve it off the floor. I found the entire episode amusing. I notice that men usually reacted to me in that manner, but did not fully understand why. During the entire evening, he was awkward and nervous, definitely not the confident, take charge person I met earlier. With a huge grin on his face, he introduced me to his male friends, who reacted to me by either hugging me, kissing my hand or remained speechless with their eyes affixed on my breasts. Johnny loved their reactions and said to them that he hit the jackpot. Throughout the evening he would not let me out of his sight. He told me that he recognized that I had hidden beauty when we met earlier, but did not realize how much. When I danced with a rather attractive Island man, Johnny stared at us throughout the entire dance and when the music ended he abruptly came over and danced with me every dance thereafter. I liked seeing him react in that manner and loved having that type of control over him. It was fun. I felt pretty and powerful. After the party, he suggested that we go to his room to have a drink, watch T.V. and talk, since the night was still young. That sounded like a good idea, so I accepted the invitation.

I had no reservations about going to his room because, throughout the evening, he had been a complete gentleman. However, shortly after being in his room and having a few drinks, he started to grope me making inappropriate sexual advances. Although I told him that I was not interested in getting intimate with him, he continued to make sexual advances. It reminded me of the times that I had to fight Shelton off during our courtship years, and I was too old for that foolishness. I then stood up and in my aggressive Harlem manner, told him to go screw himself, that he had insulted me by thinking I was an easy lay, instructed him not to speak to me again, and abruptly left his room.

The next day, he saw us at the pool, said hello to Ma and Karen and tried to apologize to me for his inappropriate behavior the night before. I reminded him that I did not want to speak with him again and asked him to get out of my face. When I returned to the room, there was a huge bouquet of flowers with a card, from Johnny, asking me to please forgive him and give him another chance. He asked if I would allow him to take the three of us out to dinner that evening. I ignored the invitation and was going to throw the flowers away, but Ma stopped me. She said they were nice and she wanted to keep them in the room until we left. For the next two days, whenever I saw him, he was alone and looked miserable. No longer did he have that confident demeanor. He looked like a sad, lost puppy. While the other members of his group were having a ball, he sat alone at the bar drinking gin and tonic. Ma continued to ask me why I refused to talk to him, but I did not tell her. She knew something had happened that really upset me, but suggested that we iron it out, because he seemed to really like me.

When I saw him the day before we were scheduled to leave, he asked me to please allow him to take us out to dinner, especially since we would be leaving the next day. Reluctantly I accepted his invitation. Ma and Karen were elated. He took us to an elegant restaurant where there was a band that played continuously during dinner. After dinner, we enjoyed the Calypso show which featured a fire eater, a person who walked on glass and limbo dancers. After the show, the band resumed playing and Karen told Johnny that she wanted to sing. Ever since she could talk, Karen loved to sing. She often entertained the family by grabbing anything that could be used as a makeshift microphone and singing a variety of songs, which always included one of my favorite songs by Millie Jackson, *Loving Arms*. Johnny spoke with the band leader who took Karen and placed her on top of the piano. He gave her a microphone and instructed her to sing whatever she wanted. As she began to sing *Loving Arms*, the band started to accompany her. Towards the end of the song, she got down on her knees and put on quite a show. The audience went wild and Karen was in her glory. Johnny had gained a friend for life, in Karen.

The following day, Johnny accompanied us to the airport and promised to call me upon his return to New York, two days later. Sure enough, he did just that and our relationship began. He treated me like a princess and constantly complimented me on my beauty. He said that he wanted me to show off my natural beauty. Those words were music to my heart. He thought I was pretty, when during my childhood I was constantly laughed at and called names because of the way I looked. He was the first person who took the time to teach me how to walk in a feminine manner and dress provocatively. Although I had made attempts to do so in the past, I never really knew whether I was doing it effectively. When he taught me some additional techniques, I became confident in my knowledge of dressing alluringly. He loved buying me nice clothes and taking me out amongst his friends. I was his show piece, which made him feel like a big shot around his friends. I enjoyed being made over and felt secure and protected by him. I was also very impressed by him. Although he was a cop, he also owned a night club in Queens. He was looked upon by his friends and acquaintances as a big shot. Whenever he took me to his club, I was treated like a queen. His staff would cater to my every wish. I imagined that was the way the women who dated the number runners on 7th Avenue felt when they were out with them. He did possess that pimp like quality that I had sensed when we first met and I made a conscious decision to accept the experience. Being with him was intriguing for about four months and then I wanted more emotion in our relationship. I wanted to be more to him than a show piece. I wanted to truly be his lady, but that never happened. Although he tried, he couldn't. He was still in love with a woman, from his past, who died in a car accident while he was driving under the influence of alcohol. He could never forget her or forgive himself. There was a sadness about him which kept me intrigued. I guess I wanted to prove to myself that I could make him love me and forget about the woman, but he never got to know the real me. I doubt whether he wanted to and he never allowed me to get close to him emotionally. I could not compete with a dead woman, and I realized that our relationship was superficial and could never become more than what it was. Eventually, I got tired of that farce of a relationship. We both knew the relationship was going nowhere, however, for some reason, neither of us would let it go. After about a year, he finally told me it was over. Although, in my heart, I knew it should end, I did not have the confidence to end it. So when he did, I cried and was so depressed that I was unable to go to work for two weeks.

Maybe I was reacting to the reality that this was another failed relationship. Rejection, betrayal and failure seemed to be the calling card for my relationships. But, when I looked at the relationships in a positive way, I saw that each allowed me to grow in one way or another. This relationship helped me to feel better about my physical self. As a result, I continued to wear high heels and clinging dresses with low cleavage, in vibrant colors. When I walked down the street or visited Caribbean Islands, I carried myself like a famous movie star and often was treated like one.

Traveling became my favorite pastime. Whenever I had enough money, I traveled to various Caribbean Islands. Barbuda had the most beautiful beaches of all. The sand was actually white, and was visible even in fairly deep water. The Palm trees against the tropical sun, blue skies, white sand and aqua green water made me think about Shelton. How I wished we could share the splendor of his home Island together. It would have been wonderful to walk hand in hand and feel the presence of our common ancestors' spirits outside the caves, which the slaves used as hiding places to escape slave owners. It was not meant to be. By then, Shelton was living with the woman who had his baby. They had another child and were working on a third. There was no way we could ever regain what we had. Too much water was under the bridge. Whenever he came to visit Karen, the longing was still visible in his eyes. I avoided looking at him. Rosetta used to look at us, shake her head and say "that's a shame." It was a shame. We were two people who loved each other but came together too soon in our lives. We both needed to first mature, experience life, and learn life's lessons. I still ached for him, but could not have him. I was able to manage on my own. His lady and other children needed him more than me and Karen, at least that's what I told myself. So the years passed, they continued to live together and I continued to muddle through doomed relationships.

Soon traveling became unsatisfying. Antigua, Barbuda, Nassau, Freeport, Bermuda, Barbados, St.Maarten, Martinique, Dominica, Puerto Rico, St. Thomas, St. Croix, St. Johns, Jamaica, Aruba, although they all had their uniqueness, they all began to look and feel the same. I felt as though I was searching for something, but was confused and did not know what it was. Then I came up with the bright idea that I wanted another child. My rationale was that Karen needed a sibling. She often said to me, when her cousins were not home or did not want to play with her, "everyone has someone except me." She said that quite often

136

and I began to take notice. Rosetta was married with two children, Nicole was married with two children, Vanessa was married with three children, Gregory was married with two children, Richie was married with one child, but that child lived with his first wife, Kevin was married with one child much younger than Karen. By now, Karen was eight years old. If I was going to have another child, it needed to be soon.

I toyed with the idea of having another child with Shelton. After all, he used to be my husband and was the father of my child. That made a lot of sense to me. I discussed my idea with Rosetta, who in her wisdom, told me that she disagreed with my idea. She told me, I was giving up and had no faith that the right man would come into my life. She would say things like "Hold on, have faith and things will work out for you. Don't make a decision that you will regret later. What could Shelton offer you. He is having a bunch of babies, is hardly able to take care of them and is not taking care of Karen. Why put yourself in that predicament?" She was right; I had given up thinking that Mr. Right was going to come into my life. I was tired of the games that were being played, even though I had been a willing participant. It was time that I got at least something that I really wanted.

Of course, I did not listen to her. I had my plan and no one was going to deter me. It was easy to ignite a sexual relationship with Shelton. He was ready, willing and able. We started seeing each other while he continued to live with his lady. In my mind, I only wanted him to impregnate me. I did not want him as my man or for any lasting romantic relationship. I knew he could not support another child and that wasn't what I wanted. I was a professional woman and financially capable of providing for my children. Any financial support from him would be gravy. Shelton had no idea of my plan. He began to become more and more engrossed in our relationship. Then he started talking about our living together and trying to make it again. That was not part of my plan. Moreover, I realized that I no longer loved him the way I did in the past. I did not trust or respect him. The mere fact that he was living with a woman and having sex with me proved that he was untrustworthy. He had hurt me deep down to my core and I could never respect or love him that way again.

One day, while we were at my apartment making passionate love, someone rang the door bell. In the nude, I reluctantly went to see who it was. I looked through the peep hole and to my surprise, there was Shelton's lady standing there calling out his name. Momentarily, I was in a state of shock but that quickly passed. I was upset that I did not have any clothes on because I wanted to go out there and kick her ass. How dare she come looking for him and ring my door bell, especially after what she did to me (having his baby and coming to my wedding). She had a long overdue ass whipping coming. Frantically, I ran into the bedroom and threw on some clothes, all the while Shelton was asking what was going on. Without answering, I ran into the kitchen and got a knife. He managed to put his pants on because he knew my temper and knew that something was terribly wrong. When I opened my door, she was already in the elevator and just as I approached it, the door closed and the elevator descended. I took the steps in hopes of reaching the ground floor before her, but by the time I got downstairs, she was pulling off in Shelton's car. I was pissed. When we got back upstairs, I lit into him. "How dare you allow that woman to know where I live." What kind of a man was he to not safeguard my privacy? I told him to take his punk ass home and never come back. I also told him to tell that bitch that "her ass is mine. She better be on the lookout for me and cross the street if she ever sees me, because if I see her first, I'm going to kick her ass." He left and we did not see each other again for a few years. He did not even come to see or call Karen. I often thought about that incident and realized that probably, in his subconscious, he wanted that to happen. He wanted to be rescued and therefore made it convenient for his lady to track him down. He was a coward, who felt trapped and did not have the courage to make a decision.

I had to tell somebody about the incident. I dare not tell Ma. Rosetta was my best bet, although I knew she was going to preach to me. That would be okay because I knew she loved me and would respect my feelings. While telling Rosetta about the incident, she listened intently and occasionally made a humming sound. We do that whenever we are pissed off and have no way of releasing the anger, so we hum. When I finished telling her the story, she said "that chic has a lot of nerve, didn't she know that she could have gotten killed." Then she started pointing out my wrongs and hoped that it was a learning experience for me. I learned that it was unfair for me to play with Shelton's love for me, and in the process disrupt a family and compromise my integrity.

DAWNING

The feeling of despair and hopelessness regarding my love life seemed to intensify. It seemed there was no one I could love and who would love me. So, I concentrated on raising Karen and advancing my career as a human services administrator. I buried myself in my work, taking no time for enjoyment. Subconsciously, I decided that I was through with men. For me to get involved again, a man would have to stand on his head to get my attention and then aggressively pursue me. No more miss nice lady. This was a tough world and I was going to be a tough lady.

My girlfriends often invited me to parties or to go to clubs, but I refused. Being in my bed alone weeping seemed more appealing, until my promiscuous friend insisted that I attend a party she was giving. If I refused, she would not speak to me again. So rather than lose her friendship, I attended the party. The place was packed and everyone seemed to be having a good time. At least it appeared that way. Upon closer observation of the people, I found that they were being phoney, acting like they were having fun but in reality, they weren't. It was a facade of loud laughter and nonsensical meaningless chatter. I wanted no part of it, so I decided to take a seat in a corner of the room and observe the spectacle. People were getting high off of a variety of substances, dancing wildly and making love to total strangers. It was rapidly turning into an orgy. After watching the nonsense for about two hours, I was ready to go back to my lonely bed. While saying my good-byes, I noticed a rather intoxicated man trying to make his way out of the door but could not stand up unassisted to accomplish that feat. When I finally got to the door to leave, I asked him whether he needed help. His reply was a slurred, yes. So, I assisted him to the elevator and as we descended, I thought, how pitiful that a man should get so intoxicated that he could not take care of himself. What could be so wrong, in his life, that would warrant wanting to be oblivious to his surroundings? A cab was waiting for him, so I put him in the cab and off he went. While driving home, I decided, no more of those meaningless parties for me, even if I lose a friend.

Three days after the party, my girlfriend called and told me that a guy, who had attended the party, was inquiring about me. I thought she had to be pulling my leg because I did not speak to or dance with anyone at that party. In fact, I secluded myself so whoever it was had to be talking about someone else. She was sure it was me by the description that he gave; very tall, slim, medium brown skin, afro, sweet and helpful. He told her how the person helped him downstairs and into his waiting cab. Well, that was me alright, but I was not interested in talking to him. She tried to tell me about him, but I was not interested. I had my own problems and did not need to get involved with another alcoholic like Arnold. One was enough in a lifetime. There wasn't anything that she could possibly tell me about him that would interest me, even if he had a million dollars. I politely ended our conversation and gave no more thought to it or him.

Two weeks later, my girlfriend called me again and told me that he had been calling her requesting my telephone number because he wanted the opportunity to thank me for helping him that night. I told her to tell him it was not necessary for him to thank me, I would have done the same thing for anybody. Two days later she called again insisting that I allow her to give him my telephone number, because he was bugging her and would not take no for an answer. She swore he was a nice guy and not Jack the Ripper. She pleaded with me to just allow him to extend his appreciation, so I gave her permission to give him my number. The next day he called. His voice was quite distinguished and intriguing. It was a big difference from his slurred speech during the party. He apologized for the condition he had been in and thanked me for being so gracious about seeing to it that he got safely to the cab. He assured me that what I had witnessed was not his normal behavior and wished to take me to dinner to prove it and to show his appreciation. An internal warning alarm went off inside me and I declined his offer.

That Saturday a bouquet of flowers were delivered to my home. Then, that Monday a bouquet of a dozen roses was delivered to my job, with a note that read, "you will continue to receive these until you at least allow me to take you to dinner." Unimpressed, I said to myself, well this is going to be an expensive venture for him. That evening he called, we talked, and I found his conversation to be quite uplifting and interesting. There was a dimension to his conversation that I never experienced in any other man. I did not know what it was or how to describe it, but it was intriguing, so I accepted his invitation to dinner.

He did not have a car and I did not ask why. Many people, who lived in Manhattan, did not have cars because public transportation was so much more convenient, especially when traveling in Midtown Manhattan. He met me at my job and I drove. Long ago I vowed to avoid using public transportation after two guys tried to snatch my handbag when I was traveling on the subway. I did not have the need to travel into Midtown often, so I generally drove wherever I went.

He had made dinner reservations at an absolutely fantastic restaurant on East 65th Street. I had never been to such an elegant place in all my life. Although the lawyer had taken me to some pretty wonderful places, they could not compare to this fantastic place. The entrance door lead us into a wonderful interior garden with a waterfall and a small pond filled with fish. We crossed a small wooden bridge which lead us into a dimly lit lobby that was decorated with plush thick rugs, stunning French Provincial chairs and the walls were adorned with expensive oil paintings. The maitre d' greeted us in a very pleasant manner and escorted us to a beautifully arranged, romantically secluded table and pulled out my chair for me to be seated. While walking to the table, I noticed that everyone in the restaurant was white and exquisitely dressed. The women wore expensive jewelry with designer dresses. The men wore expensive suits and ties. The place was breath-taking. I had no idea that a place like this existed. This was a far cry from the restaurants I frequented in Harlem and the Bronx. I was trying hard not to show my amazement. I did not want him to think I was not used to coming to places like this. When I noticed my menu did not have prices on it, I knew he was going to pay a pretty penny for this date. I wondered whether his menu had prices on it, but dared not ask. Obviously, very rich people came here. I began to think that maybe I should have listened to what my girlfriend had to say about him after all. He had to have quite a bit of money to afford to dine at a place like this. I made a mental note to call my friend and get the scoop on him after the date.

He was quite comfortable in this environment and seemed to have come here before. He selected the wine and made recommendations regarding food selections. I chose a shrimp dish. He ate fish. The food was tasty , but the portions were too small. Restaurants that I frequented filled your plate with food. We had an assortment of different desserts and enjoyed selecting them. I drank one glass of wine and he finished the bottle of wine and ordered cognac after the meal. Our conversation was pleasant. He worked for a not-for-profit organization in Harlem as the Director of one of its programs. I too worked in Harlem and directed a program for " at risk" youth. Interestingly, he had also grown up in Harlem, however, I could not relate to some of the things, like the type of music, dance steps and other forms of entertainment, he had experienced since he was fourteen years older than me. As he spoke, that puzzling, strange quality that intrigued me during our telephone conversation surfaced again. It was how he spoke, his choice of calming words and his pleasant jovial manner. There was a care free air about him, as if he was worry free. I felt comfortable with him and found myself expressing opinions about various subjects quite freely. He was a good listener and seemed genuinely interested in my opinions. When we were ready to leave, he paid the bill in cash and gave me money for gas. I dropped him off at the Harlem YMCA where he said he played basketball and I continued home to the Bronx. Charles was an interesting and mysterious person whom I wanted to get to know better.

As the weeks went by, we saw a great deal of each other; often eating lunch together, going to the movies and going to more nice restaurants for dinner. I noticed that he would have drinks every time we ate, even during lunch. When he visited me at home, he always brought a bottle of liquor, which he would just about finish all by himself, since I only drank occasionally. One day he convinced me to accompany him to a lecture to hear an inspirational speaker. Aside from the time that Constance Baker Motley had spoken at my Junior High School, I had not heard anyone else talk about endless possibilities and self determination, so I was intrigued with the speaker's uplifting message. I suddenly realized that was the strange intriguing characteristic that attracted me to Charles. I had never met anyone who talked about possibilities, self determination, reaching for the moon and spiritual growth. Once, while laying in bed together, after making fantastic love, he told me that he was going to be a millionaire. He said it so confidently, I had no doubt that he would. It did not dawn on me to ask him how he planned to achieve his goal, I just believed him. He was so encouraging and because he helped me to see my real potential, I had no reason to doubt what he said. The sky was the limit and I could do anything I put my mind to.

Where had he been all of my life. I needed him around some years earlier, when I was too afraid to pursue law school, since I had been discouraged by professionals twice in my life. He would have encouraged me to become a successful lawyer, instead of settling for obtaining a master's degree in social work. Whether he was just full of hot air with no action, remained to be seen. All I knew was that he made me feel good about myself. Within four months, our relationship grew tremendously. Aside from doing a lot of things together, we talked with each other about everything. Time seemed to slip away while we were together. Although I did not have a burning love for him, I liked him a lot and appreciated his interest in me. We were happy being together. I looked forward to seeing him because we shared quality time together. For the first time in a very long time, I genuinely had fun being with a man. He accepted me for who I was. I did not feel as though I had to pretend around him. The only real concern I had about him was his drinking.

I felt that he drank a bit too much, but he disagreed. Even the fact that he was a married man did not concern me as much or impact our relationship. I respected his time limitations and was quite satisfied with the quality and amount of time we spent together. I had no desire to marry him, although we began to discuss the idea of having a child together. He was elated with the idea because he only had two girls and wanted a boy.

By our sixth month of seeing each other, we began to seriously plan to have a child. There was no doubt in our minds that it would be a boy. I was always aware of when I was ovulating and got pregnant during the first month of trying. Intuition told me that this was going to be a special child. I felt the fluttering inside me when I conceived and as the child grew in my womb, I grew more excited and anxious for him to be born. However, shortly after informing Charles that we had succeeded with our plan, he became more and more distant, spending less and less time with me and when he did come over to see me, he was drunk. He had become distant and I could not reach him. One evening while we were at a bar with his friends, he went to the bathroom and his closest friend approached me and told me that Charles was experiencing a great deal of stress regarding my pregnancy. I asked him whether it was his idea to speak to me or did Charles ask him to tell me. He fumbled around with a response. Without saying a word, I left the bar and went home. Charles tried calling me several times that night, but I was too angry to answer the phone. How dare he be stressed and not share his concerns with me? Instead he talked to his friend. Wasn't I his friend? Didn't he feel comfortable enough to be honest with me? We could have worked it out together. Was that why I saw less and less of him? It seemed like my world was coming to an end. With his positive thinking and reassuring manner, I thought that Charles could handle anything and would always be there for me, even if we never got married. I liked and cared about him and never thought that he too would disappoint and abandon me. Here again was another man who proved to me that I could not trust him. That night I made up my mind that I would have my baby without him. He could keep his stressed ass with his wife. I did not care. In the back of my mind, my conscience was saying, you got what you deserved. What did you expect from a married man? You reap what you sow.

There I was again carrying another child without the benefit of the father's love and attention. But, I did not feel sorry for myself. I was having the child I planned to have. It was exciting. Of course, Charles made a few lame attempts to see me, but I brushed him off. He wanted to know what happened and I told him that he did not have to send his friend with a message from him to me. He could have been a man and told me himself. I told him that I had no respect for him and refused to be aggravated by a man who had no balls to stand by his decision and responsibility. What about all that talk about doing and being so much? I found out it was all hot air. My initial gut reaction, when we had our first telephone conversation, was warning me to back off, but I didn't, so I got what I deserved.

The birth of Kamal was truly eventful. Rosetta was in the delivery room with me as my coach. She tried to persuade me to have natural birth, but I wanted drugs. As usual I insisted on doing it my way so I insisted that the doctor give me drugs one hour prior to his birth, after going through fourteen hours of labor. I just could not take the pain anymore. After receiving the drugs, I felt like I was floating on cloud nine and completely forgot about the fact that I was in labor. I no longer felt the contractions, therefore, I did not know when to push. The doctor began to yell at me, the baby was in distress and I needed to push. Rosetta slapped my face and told me to wake up and push. I started pushing, but at the wrong time. I didn't know what I was doing. Rosetta told the doctor to tell her when I needed to push and she would slap me and I would push. That's how I delivered Kamal. My everlasting and reliable sister-friend had helped me bring another prized possession into this world. This time it was my boy child.

He was a darling little boy with a funny face and freckles. When he smiled his long giant dimples consumed his cheeks. He looked like his father. For the next four years, I was totally engrossed in caring for my two children. Karen was elated that she finally had someone too. She was a great help with her brother. I had no time to think about any men. I was too busy raising my children and elevating my career. Life was interesting. I looked forward to returning home each day to my wonderful children. Each night we read together, played games and talked.

Who needed a man? I mean, who needed the types of

men I found myself with time and time again. I wanted a man in my life whom I loved and who really loved me for me; not for my body, nor as a showpiece, not for sex, and not as a sounding board to listen to his hopes and dreams. Instead to be loved, appreciated, handled with care, and share our lives together as a couple building and supporting each other in all of our endeavors. That's all I ever wanted in a relationship. I began to question whether it was possible for me to meet someone like that. I made up my mind to hold on and wait for that special someone to come into my life. However, there was something way back in my mind, a very faint inaudible voice, trying to tell me something that I could not understand. I knew it had something to do with the kind of thinking Charles did. It had to do with self-determination, self-esteem, self-love and self-respect. But there was more. Something beyond me, but I couldn't put my finger on it. It started to taunt me. Soon I became restless, as though I needed to do something beyond what I was doing. I began to think that I needed to change careers, do something different, more exciting. I was groping at straws, not knowing what to do about my restlessness.

An opportunity presented itself for me to become involved in another career. Since childhood, I was always fascinated with the entertainment field. Although I never wanted to be a performer, I felt I had a natural talent for producing, directing and promoting. So when an opportunity presented itself for me and some of my siblings to produce, direct and promote two shows featuring my brother Gregory and Mrs. Kates' three daughters, who used to sing at our house with Gregory's band, we accepted the challenge. I quit my job and devoted my time and money to the production of a mini musical. Rosetta, Nicole, Kevin, Laura and I worked diligently to put the production together. Gregory was starring in the production. He always loved to perform as a comedian and singer. We helped him cultivate his singing talents. We worked tirelessly to produce the show and it was a success. It was an event to remember. The show was held at the Cotton Club in Harlem. We had promoted it as an "Evening of Elegance" and attendance was by invitation only. We all knew a lot of very interesting people who were more than happy to pay the price to attend the affair. They arrived in limousines, and other luxury cars, many of which were rented for the evening. Women were dressed in fashionable gowns and men in tuxedos. They were people from all walks of life including doctors, lawyers, businessmen, politicians, teachers, entertainers, radio personalities, number runners, etc. They all came prepared to spend a lot of money and have a good time, which they did. Champagne was flowing like water and before the affair was over, much to the surprise of the Cotton Club manager, all of the liquor had been sold out. Once we realized that we could be successful at producing shows, we wrote, directed and produced another show. It too was a success. We were then faced with making decisions about our futures. Did we want to pursue this field or resume our other careers?

By that time, Nicole, Laura and Gregory had already decided to leave the business because they were not willing to invest the time and hard work. We also had difficulty working out our differences, so they decided to take their profits and leave. Rosetta, Kevin and I were faced with making a decision. It was a difficult decision, since we had a minimal amount of money to invest in our company. We decided to test the waters one more time by producing another show, but with a different twist. Instead of a Rhythm and Blues show like the other two, we decided to produced a show with a Jazz theme. It turned out to be a flop, so that was the determining factor. I could not continue, since I needed to work to support my family. Having used all of my savings and with no other means of support, I had to face reality and get a job. Rosetta and Kevin also had financial obligations to their families. Reluctantly, we dissolved our promotional company.

Not knowing what I wanted to do, I felt even more isolated and lost. I had a strong urge to get away from it all. For a few years, I had been toying with the idea of relocating, just moving out of New York, but I did not know where I wanted to live. I was feeling overwhelmed and out of control. I needed to get away and think about my future, so when a friend of mine told me about a trip that she was organizing to St.Thomas, Virgin Islands, I decided to go. Rosetta went along with me because she needed a vacation before starting a new teaching position. I intended to rest, relax, clear my head and begin to make plans for my future. Rosetta, on the other hand wanted to party. Whenever we traveled together, we always stayed together to avoid any problems that might occur in a strange land. So needless to say, I had to go with Rosetta to the parties.

Every Heart Knows Its Own Sorrow

During the second day of the trip, after returning from the beach, we showered, dressed and went downstairs to the patio of the hotel where a calypso band played every evening after five. I was in no mood for that scene. All I wanted to do was go to my room and sleep but I could not abandon Rosetta, so I reluctantly sat at the corner of the bar and ordered a tasty Pina Colada. Rosetta was dancing and having a wonderful time. I, on the other hand, had refused several requests for dances and preferred to wallow in my drink. Then just as I was really getting quite comfortable, sitting by myself and enjoying my second Pina Colada, I heard a man's voice ask me whether the seat next to me was vacant. Without looking at him I replied, "I do not see anyone sitting there, do you?" He chuckled and proceeded to sit in the seat. Then he asked if I would buy him a drink. Slowly I lifted my head tilting it towards him and said, "I was just about to ask you the same thing." He chuckled again and said, "no problem," and without hesitating ordered two more Pina Coladas for me and a ginger ale for himself. Looking at him I thought to myself, "oh, a wise guy." I was not in the mood to play any games, so I asked him what was he trying to prove ordering two Pina Coladas for me. He said something to the effect that he wanted me to know that it was no problem for him to order whatever and as much as I wanted. If he was trying to impress me, I was not impressed. I decided that I would drink the two Pina Coladas and ignore anymore of his advances, which I did. He tried to talk to me and I ignored him. So he stopped talking to me. He just sat there and I just sat there. The music was sounding great and

Rosetta was having a ball dancing with everyone who asked her to dance. He must have noticed my feet tapping and my body moving in my seat, because eventually he asked me to dance, but I refused.

Rosetta finally came back to the bar with a big grin on her face. She said hello to him and asked me why I had two Pina Coladas in front of me. Before I could answer, he asked her if she cared for a drink and she told him that she would love to have a Pina Colada. I started to tell her that she could have one of mine, but he interrupted and said, "those are yours, she can have her own." Rosetta turned slowly to me with a knowing grin on her face and said "I guess he told you." Then she started gesturing to me asking "who is he?" I shrugged my shoulders responding, "I don't know." She then turned to him and introduced herself and introduced me. He then pulled out two of his business cards, giving one to each of us, and introduced himself. I did not bother to read it. When the bartender brought Rosetta's drink, she thanked him and proposed a toast saying, "here's to us, St.Thomas and a good time." He tapped his glass on hers and I reluctantly picked up my drink and touched each of their glasses with mine.

The band started playing one of my favorite songs, *Shiny Eyes* and Rosetta said, "Carol, there's your song." Someone came over and asked her to dance. Another guy was approaching to ask me to dance but our new friend, Ellis, made eye contact with the guy who quickly turned around. I was amazed to see the guy scamper at the sight of Ellis. Who was he anyway? How dare he bully men away from me? He then turned to me and asked me to dance. I could not resist dancing to that song, so I accepted. Ellis was not my type, he was shorter than I with a big round belly and he wore out of style clothes. However, he did have broad shoulders and could dance very well. In fact, I rather enjoyed dancing with him. He seemed quite confident in himself. Moreover, he was not too pushy. I appreciated him not forcing a conversation, when it was obvious, I did not feel like talking. While dancing, he commented on how well I danced calypso and asked where I learned how to dance like that, since I was obviously from the States. I told him that my parents were West Indian and I grew up on that music. He then took me in his arms and started really whining his hips, as if to say, ok lets do it. We had a ball dancing together. By the end of the evening, I was actually laughing and talking.

Rosetta had run into the husband of her friend, who asked if we wanted to go to a club later. He was going to pick up his wife, and we all could go and party. Ellis asked me if I would go with him to the club, and I responded that I would prefer that we all travel together. He was not happy with that idea and suggested that the rest of us go ahead and have a good time. Ellis did not show up at the club that night and I was somewhat disappointed. Although I danced with other guys, it was not as much fun as I had dancing with Ellis. When we got back to the hotel, Rosetta took a look at Ellis' business card. She pointed out to me that he held a rather impressive political position in the Virgin Islands Government. I shrugged and said that's nice, but he is not my type. Rosetta replied, "but he makes you laugh."

The next morning while eating breakfast, Ellis came and asked us what we planned to do that day. I was secretly happy to see him, but acted nonchalantly and replied that we probably would go to the beach. He asked if we would allow him to drive us to a wonderful beach, but he would not be able to stay. He had business to take care of, but would pick us up later and take us to lunch. I hesitated so Rosetta quickly accepted graciously. He got up and told us he would be right back. We saw him motion to the waitress, pull out some money, give it to her and leave. I noticed that she acted as though she was afraid of him because of his abrupt manner. In fact, I sensed that people were afraid of him and he seemed to be mean to them. However, he treated me totally different. He was particularly gentle and kind to me. So I relaxed and enjoyed it. He returned about ten minutes later, with a big smile on his face and beckoned us to come. When we called the waitress, she informed us that everything had been taken care of. From that point until we had to leave two days later, we had a ball. Ellis had arranged for us to go on tours of the Island. Our evenings were filled with good food and interesting places to dance and listen to great music. He chauffeured us everywhere.

On the last day, when he drove us to the airport, we both were feeling badly that I had to leave. He asked me to stay, but I couldn't. I had to get back to my children and begin looking for a job. As we said our good-byes, I noticed that he was uncharacteristically somber. I was surprised, since I had gotten the impression that he was always in control of

Every Heart Knows Its Own Sorrow

his emotions. When I got back home, he called at least once a week.

Two months had passed and my job search was not going well, mostly because I was not sure what I wanted to do. I shared my dilemma with Ellis, who listened intently to my confusion and suggested that I come to St.Thomas and look for a job. I informed him that I would not want to live on St.Thomas because of the hills and congestion, but would consider living on St.Croix. He said that he would speak to some people he knew who might be able to help me find a job. So I went back to St.Thomas and spent a week looking for a job. Since St.Thomas is the capital of the US Virgin Islands, I was able to conduct my search for a government job on St. Croix from there. While there, Ellis and I got to know each other better. He was compassionate, responsible and assertive. He seemed to have everything under control. He rented a three level home for me to stay in during that time, arranged for my interviews and drove me to them. After the interviews, he took me to the beach, then to eat and then back to the house, where I abruptly fell asleep. He did not disturb me. I felt as though the weight of the world was on my shoulders and all I wanted to do was sleep. It seemed he understood. I remembered awakening one evening and observed him standing in the doorway of the bedroom gazing at me. Although in a sleepy haze, I managed to apologize for sleeping all of the time and then fell back to sleep. Each night he made sure that the house was securely locked and, when satisfied that I was all right, left. I felt safe and assured that I did not have to worry about anything.

During my awake hours, we laughed and talked a lot. He introduced me to his mother and other family members who seemed to be nice, friendly people. His mother prepared a delicious supper for us one evening, which consisted of fish in gravy, peas and rice, plantains, roasted turkey wings, potato stuffing and cabbage. After eating such a hearty meal, that night I slept like a log. Aside from introducing me to his family, he also told me about his wife. He explained that they lived together and there was no reason for him to leave. Although they could be happier, they were okay. I was not phased by him being married because I did not love him and did not want to marry him. If I lived on St.Croix, we would not see much of each other anyway. All I wanted from him was friendship.

One month after that trip, I was offered a job on St.Croix. I was excited, but Karen was upset and did not want to leave her friends. Kamal did not care one way or the other; Ma was concerned about me going so far away with no friends or family to depend on; and Rosetta was quiet. The night before I left, all of my siblings came over and helped me pack. We played music, told jokes and tried to hold back the tears. I was the first one to move out of New York. Richie had gone into the service, but that was different. I was moving 1600 miles away. Ma had become close to my children and often referred to them as hers, so it was particularly difficult for her to allow them leave. Afraid of being left alone without my children to keep her company, she suggested that I leave the children with her until I got situated, but I would not consider it. Where I went, my children went, and still Rosetta said nothing. Ellis had gotten a trailer home for me and the children. I had no idea how it looked or where it was located on the Island. I trusted him and knew that I could depend on him to work everything out, properly. Ma did not know him and was very skeptical about me taking my children into such uncertainty. I was adventurous and Rosetta was still quiet.

It was difficult saying good-bye to my family and friends. My long time drinking and hang out partner Lloyd came over that night and scolded me about abandoning him and taking his Goddaughter away from him. I told him that it only meant that we had new territory where we could hang out. He thought about it and agreed. He promised to visit as soon as I got settled. As everyone left that night, we hugged and cried. It seemed we cried a river of tears. Rosetta and her family were the last to leave. Her husband, Delwood, said he didn't know how he was going to deal with her, now that I was leaving. He shook his head, gave me a kiss and said "sis, take care of yourself and those kids." Rosetta was the last to leave. Throughout the evening, she silently helped me pack without looking at me. As she approached the door where I was standing, I noticed that her eyes were filled with tears that were on the verge of rolling down her cheeks. When she finally looked at me, it was as though a damn had busted releasing a constant flow of tears. I had dreaded this moment because I knew how she was feeling. I felt like I was deserting my best friend. We embraced for the first time in our lives. We never had a reason to hug each other before because we were always there for each other and together all

160

the time. Now I was going away and it felt strange to think that I was leaving my life long sister-buddy-friend behind. Tears were insufficient to express what we were feeling. I was there for her all of her life. We were each others support, friend, and confidant. How do you turn that loose gracefully? With tear filled eyes, Rosetta whispered in my ear, "I love you Carol, take care of yourself." Without turning back, she left. That moment I knew that although we would always have a loving spiritual connection, our relationship would never be the same. I felt like, for the first time in our lives, we would be on our own and would truly grow up by being apart. I felt sad and excited at the same time. I was sad about leaving my family, friends and everything I had known all of my life. I especially felt sad about leaving Rosetta alone. Aside from Delwood and me, Rosetta had no friends. I was her buddy and spiritual friend. It was hard leaving her. Yet, I also felt excited because I was embarking on an adventure, something new and different. It was exciting to think about entering the unknown. Ellis was waiting for me and my children and I had no doubt that he would help us through. We were going to need his help because I had no idea how it would be living on an Island. Aside from going to camp every summer, during my childhood, I knew nothing about country life. I grew up in the concrete jungle, in one of the busiest cities in the world. We were going to have to learn how to live in an entirely new environment and culture.

I thought about Grandma and imagined that she must have had much more trepidation than I when she made the journey to America all by herself. I began to feel Grandma's strength and became more determined to succeed. If Grandma did it by herself, then surely I could do it with the help of my children and Ellis. At least I had a job lined up that would provide me with a decent income. Grandma had no skills and had to search for a low paying job. If she was able to survive under those circumstances, then surely I could also.

The next day could not come soon enough. I did not sleep at all that night. All kinds of thoughts were racing through my mind. Did I pack everything? Were we going to be on time to catch the plane? Will the home be comfortable? I felt somewhat badly for Karen because she had started high school and had to leave all of her friends and cousins. However, she was beginning to concern me. Occasionally, she would not come home directly after school and her grades had started to worsen. I anticipated that the change would probably do her good.

The next morning, I woke the kids up bright and early. I wanted to make sure that we would be on time to catch the plane. A friend of mine had offered the use of his van to transport us to the airport, since we had so many things. It was quite hectic getting everything checked in at the airport. By the time we boarded the plane, I felt as though I had done a full day's work. Sweat was pouring off of me. Karen did a wonderful job keeping an eye on Kamal, who, in his excitement wanted to explore everything in the airport. We all were excited while boarding the airplane. Karen had flown only a few times and this was Kamal's second time on an airplane. He was only two years old when we visited St.

Croix before and did not remember flying, so he asked a million questions which Karen and I took turns answering.

When we landed in St. Croix, I became quite anxious to see Ellis. I was looking all around while waiting at the baggage area. He was nowhere to be found. I began to panic. Did he have a change of heart? Was he going to leave us stranded without anyplace to go? Then, he approached me from behind and gave me a huge hug, all the while laughing and saying, "You thought I wouldn't come, didn't you? I told you that I will always be here for you, you can depend on me." He turned to Kamal, rubbed his head and said, "this must be Kamal, hi young man, and this beautiful young lady must be Karen." Kamal inched closer to me and refused to let my hand go. He never spoke to strangers and was not about to start. Karen gave a weak smile and proceeded to retrieve the luggage. Ellis had brought a few men to help with our things. He instructed Karen to just point out our belongings and the men would take care of the rest. Karen gave me a quizzical look as if to ask, who does he think he is? We rode with Ellis while the men followed in a truck. I felt very special and for the first time in weeks, relaxed. I knew that Ellis would take care of everything.

Our trailer home was located in a place called "Peppertree" which was located next to an outdoor theater called "Island Center." The trailer home was cozy. I had never been in one before and was amazed that it was like an apartment inside. It had two bedrooms, two bathrooms, a kitchen and a living room. Although it was not spacious, it was comfortable. It had a long porch and plenty of yard space for Kamal to play. I was satisfied with the arrangements that Ellis had made. Although Karen did not say anything, I knew she liked what she saw. Kamal was already running around outside. Living in the city, he never had the opportunity to run around in clean grass.

Although it was hot, there was a breeze that blew. We had two Palm trees and a Mahogany tree that surrounded our trailer home. This felt like home. Ellis went outside and started playing with Kamal, while Karen and I talked and cleaned. She did admit to liking the house and was amazed that there were two bathrooms. After we cleaned and put most of our things away, we all took a tour of the trailer park. There were about forty trailer homes in the park, a laundry area, playground, club house and swimming pool. It was located down the road from two supermarkets, a hospital and a shopping center. We were impressed. Ellis took us food shopping and bought the kids swimming gear for the beach. For dinner, he took us out for Pizza, which really earned him brownie points with the kids. He then took them to the Island Center where the "Fat Boys" were in concert. Karen could not believe what was happening and started to become more friendly towards Ellis. Kamal had already accepted Ellis as a friend and was even showing him his break dancing skills, which were quite uncoordinated. For the first time, I felt like my family was complete.

Ellis remained with us for the rest of the week. His job required him to work on both St. Thomas and St. Croix, so we were going to see quite a bit of each other. He was going to be with us at least three days a week. Although I had not anticipated seeing him so often, it was fine with me especially since the kids liked him. I enrolled Karen and Kamal in a private school, which they loved. They both made friends quickly and Karen seemed to think less about the friends she left behind. I was not scheduled to start work for another two weeks, so while the kids were in school, I acquainted myself with the various parts of the Island. Ellis had given me a car and helped me adjust to driving on the left hand side of the road. Once I got the hang of it, I preferred it to driving on the right.

 Every weekend we went to the beach, which was fifteen minutes away from our home. In New York we seldom went to beaches because they were so far away, crowded and the water looked dirty. When I started traveling to the Islands, I stopped going to the beaches in New York completely. They no longer qualified, in my mind, to be called beaches.

 Living on the Island, life seemed carefree and easy. Most of all, I loved sitting on the porch at night and gazing at the beautiful Caribbean star filled sky. Only in the Caribbean had I seen such a beautiful sky and felt the pleasant tropical evening breeze. I felt closer to nature and at peace with the world. My soul and spirit were happy. I wanted to capture the beauty that I saw. A strong urge to paint overtook me. Although I was not an artist, I wanted to express and share with the world what I saw. So, I tried my hand at painting, but quickly realized that painting was not my forte. Karen was kind and encouraged me to continue practicing, but I knew that it was futile. There had to be another way that I could share my joy with the world. Since I had no idea what that was, I just continued to enjoy those experiences for myself.

One afternoon, while the kids were still at school and before I started my job, Ellis came over to see me. He brought some soup, salt fish and Johnny Cakes for lunch. The food was quite tasty. Although my mother prepared Johnny Cakes, these were different. They consisted of the same ingredients: flour, oil, water, salt and baking powder, but these were fluffier. While I was washing the dishes, Ellis came behind me and kissed my neck. Although we had kissed before, this felt different. It felt as though he wanted to do more. Just then my song, *Shiny Eyes* started to play on the radio. Holding me around my waist, he started whining his body to the rhythm of the music. I loved the way he whined and could not resist whining in unison with him. Soon our bodies where moving together in sensual gyrations. I could no longer resist his warm kisses and strong arms around my waist. I seemed to melt in his arms as he picked me up and carried me into the bedroom and gently placed me on the bed. He made love to me, while telling me how beautiful I was and how he was going to always take care of me. I felt safe with him and allowed myself to relax and enjoy making love. It had been a long time since I made love. It felt liberating and soon I expressed my feelings for him and he displayed his satisfaction over and over again.

That was the beginning of our love affair. No longer were we just friends. We became family. I was still alright with knowing that he was married. In my mind, I was happy with our relationship the way it was. We saw each other often, just enough not to get on each other's nerves. The children liked him and he treated them as though they were his. Life was good. We did everything together. When he took us to the beach, we spent hours having fun playing water football. Karen and I against Ellis and Kamal. During carnival, we got up at 4:00am and drove Karen and her friends to participate in jourvert morning celebrations. I could not believe that people got out of their beds in the wee hours of the morning to dance and have sex in the streets. Karen was becoming quite a dancer and enjoyed it immensely. Prior to moving to St. Croix, she did not know how to dance Soca or Calypso. Now she was whining more than me. Kamal was bored with the whole ordeal and preferred to sleep in the back of the car.

Carnival was one of many cultural events that took place every year. Another one, that Kamal liked, was the Bull and Bread event, where various farm animals and the local harvests were on display. People were given Bull and Bread to eat along with other tasty dishes. Kamal would not eat the food, but enjoyed looking at the animals. We all started to feel like St.Croix was our home and began to think less about New York.

Ma and Rosetta stayed in constant contact with me. We talked on the telephone at least twice a week. Ma was missing us and wanted to visit. She came to St.Croix three months after we had moved there. She had never been to St. Croix, although she traveled extensively to Africa, South America, Europe and other Caribbean Islands. When she went inside the trailer home, she smiled and said it was cute. However, she was most anxious to meet Ellis. Ma arrived on a Wednesday and Ellis was not due on St.Croix until Friday. So we had two days to chat and for her to fill me in on the happenings back home. We talked for hours about everything and anything. She was elated to see the children and gave them big hugs when they came home from school. She could not believe that Kamal was beginning to gain weight, since he was a finicky eater and refused most foods. Karen had also begun to gain weight. She loved the Caribbean food and ate anything we put in front of her. Ma even commented on how good I looked and could not resist telling me that I seemed to be gaining weight as well.

Although we were looking well, Ma looked drawn and unhappy. She was losing weight and often repeated herself during our conversations. I also noticed that she was not as energetic. Her steps were slower and more deliberate as though she was trying to avoid falling. Rosetta told me that Ma had fallen once, in the street, and was bed ridden for a week. She convinced me that Ma had recovered, was doing fine and there was nothing to worry about. After seeing Ma for myself, I was worried. However, a few days with us and she seemed to be her old self again. She regained her energy, her appetite was good and she was amazed to see me cooking. While in New York, I rarely cooked and when I did it was usually fast food like burgers, hot dogs and canned foods. However, while on St.Croix, Ellis had taught me how to cook various Caribbean dishes, which I cooked well. He did not like fast food, so I cooked fresh wholesome meals. Each weekend we went to various locations, shopping for food. We went along Centerline Road at Sunny Isles and bought okra, tomatoes, avocados and other vegetables from the road side vendors. Then we drove along Centerline Road heading toward Freddricksted. Along the way we would stop at other road side vendors and purchase marvi, ginger beer, mangos and other fruit. At the wharf in Freddricksted, we would buy a variety of freshly caught fish. Then we would go to our favorite bakery and buy freshly baked breads, buns, pastries and sharp cheese. On our way back home, we stopped at another road side vendor and bought home made ice cream for the children. It was a weekly outing the whole family enjoyed.

The day that Ma had been waiting for had finally come. She was going to meet Ellis, the man she had heard so much about. Kamal could not stop talking about Ellis. He told her how Ellis took him to the dock where his friends were, and had him show them his break dancing skills. They gave him money for dancing, which he decided to save. His plan was to lend the money to his sister and charge her interest. As a very young child, Kamal was always good with math. Math was his favorite subject in school. When he learned the value of money, he became even more proficient in his mathematical calculations.

Ellis arrived after work. He brought Ma a bouquet of flowers and a beautiful, rather large, hand made peasant doll, which he had specially made for her. She was flabbergasted. That took her totally by surprise. She could tell that the doll was very expensive. It was quite thoughtful of him to bring her gifts. When she got over the shock, I saw her suspiciousness resurface. They made light conversation, and for the first time since I knew him, Ellis seemed nervous. He fidgeted in the chair and became preoccupied playing with Kamal. I knew he was trying to make a good impression on Ma. I had told him a lot about her, especially about her disapproval of me bringing the children here. He felt that if he met with her disapproval, she might be able to persuade me to return to New York. Since the afternoon when we first made love, we became a major part of his life. Each week he anxiously awaited the days when he could return to his St. Croix family. At that point in his life, he could not envision his life without us. We felt the same about him. Even Karen accepted his role in our lives.

Ma continued to observe him throughout the evening. It was as though she was trying to find a reason not to like him, but couldn't find one. Then she asked him about his wife and family on St. Thomas. How long was he planning on carrying on in this manner, knowing that he had a wife? Someone was bound to get hurt in this type of situation. She was concerned that it would be me. He responded in a thoughtful, sincere manner and explained that it was not his intention to hurt anyone. He had not anticipated falling in love with me and the children, and did not know what the future held. He only knew that he was not willing to give me up.

Although I was satisfied with his answer, Ma was not. Both of us had experienced being hurt by married men and she did not want to see me go through that again. So she began telling him about me. My soft vulnerable personality, giving qualities and genuine niceness. She explained that she had seen me get hurt and disappointed time and time again and did not want to see it happen in this relationship. She expressed her concern about me and the children being on St. Croix with no family or close friends to watch out for us. Ellis assured her that he made sure we were being cared for even when he was not on the Island. He had asked a number of his friends to look out for us during his absence. It was true, there were several of his friends who would call me and come by to make sure that we were ok. They were always polite and willing to assist us if we needed assistance. Once, the car malfunctioned and one of his friends took me to and from work, for a week, until the car was repaired. Other friends brought us fish, vegetables and other items, whenever they could. He assured her that he would do everything within his power to make me and the children happy. Obviously, he had convinced Ma, because she did not ask anymore questions. She saw how happy we all were and decided to enjoy her stay.

She stayed for six weeks and seemed reluctant to leave. During her stay, we had a ball going to the beach, eating out, visiting friends, going to the movies, the market, tours, etc. She enjoyed herself immensely. I enjoyed having her around and appreciated knowing that she was there with the children while I was at work. Although Karen was trustworthy, there were a few of the Island boys who liked her and wanted to visit her during my absence. Kamal made sure that I knew whenever they came around. Karen entertained them on the porch, because she knew that she could not have company when I was not at home. With Ma being there, I did not worry about what was going on at home. Although Ma liked St.Croix, she found it to be too rural and restricting. She did not like the idea of being on an Island and having to depend on an airplane or boat to get off. Without many places to go, she soon became bored. She was a big city person and after six weeks, needed more of a variety of places to see and go. It was difficult saying good-bye again. We wanted her to stay and she wanted us to leave. Neither of us wanted what the other wanted, so she had to return to New York alone.

Ellis did not go to the airport with us. He knew that I wanted to spend that time with Ma and for us to say our good-byes. We all were in tears as we hugged Ma and told her how much we loved her. We had no idea when we would see her again and were crying as though it would be the last. Although Ma had a comfortable income from Daddy's pension, it would not allow her to travel to St.Croix as often as we would like. When Ma was boarding the plane, we went on the upper level of the airport terminal and watched until the airplane disappeared from site. When she left, I felt empty and sad inside because even while we were saying goodbye, Ma did not tell me that she loved me. While we hugged, I noticed that she seemed to want to push me away from her, as though she felt uncomfortable holding me so close. I often wondered why she would never tell her children that she loves us, or hug us. Was it that Grandma never hugged her or told her that she was loved? Did she not realize that it was good to embrace your children and tell them that you love them? At that moment, I embraced my children and vowed to always tell them that I loved them, as often as possible.

HEALING

The life line

GROWTH

The transition from living in one of the busiest cities in the world to a small Caribbean Island had its ups and downs. The first adjustment for me was learning how to slow down and to move and work at a slower pace. When I first moved to St.Croix, I did everything in a hurried fashion. I was so accustomed to moving and working at a fast pace because that's how things are done in New York. People walk, talk, think and work quickly in New York, so when I moved to St. Croix I had to go through a metamorphosis. Everything was different from what I was accustomed. People actually greeted each other in the morning, despite whether they knew each other. That did not happen in New York, there we were wary of strangers. While walking down the street in St.Croix, I had to learn how not to clutch my handbag the way I did in New York. In the City, I was in constant fear that it would be snatched. I had to learn that the chance of my handbag being snatched in St.Croix was very slim. During those days, in 1984, that type of crime seldomly occurred there. One day while walking with one of my co-worker she asked me why was I walking so fast and holding onto my pocketbook like someone was going to take it. I had not noticed that I was doing those things, until she brought them to my attention. So, I had to become more aware of my body language and the messages I was inadvertently communicating. The people I worked with would often remind me that they did not work so quickly there and I would either have to slow down or take longer breaks to allow them time to catch up with me. I realized that I was making them feel uncomfortable and decided to cut down on the number of hours I spent in the office. Instead, I spent more time in the community getting acquainted with the various political, social and community organizations on the Island. By doing that I gained a more complete understanding of the culture and people, which enhanced my relationship with my co-workers. As a supervisor, I found that the people who worked for me expected me to be class conscious and treat them as subservient. Although they expected to be treated in that manner, my upbringing did not allow me to think of people in that way. I view all people as equal, even in the work place. Although we have different levels of responsibilities, everyone's duties are important. I often use the example of the janitor's role in the overall operations. If there was no janitor, everyone working in that environment would be uncomfortable. The type of work that one does is not an indication of one's character, and in my opinion, a person's character is most important. I had very good role models who demonstrated the importance of this quality.

When I think about Grandma, who was of great character, I know that my thinking is correct. Although her employers only saw her as a mere cleaning lady, it was their loss that they did not take the time to get to know her as the kind, unselfish, loving person that she was. So, I prefer to treat people as people and not judge them by their job functions, but instead by their character. As a result, I was readily accepted and respected. Ellis, on the other hand, was very class conscious and treated most people as subservient to him. He was rude, insulting and mean to most people, but he never treated me or my children in that manner. At home, he was always sensitive and fun loving. Although he was not a kind person, he was a giving person. Other people disliked and feared him because he used his authority as a weapon and wielded it as often as he deemed necessary. He and I had many long and heated discussions about the way he treated people. It made me feel uncomfortable when we would go out and he would treat people in a mean, disrespectful manner with no regard for their feelings. His response to me was that I was a bleeding heart and that's why people tended to take advantage of me.

In an environment that did not readily accept outsiders, I found that my family and I were welcomed, once the Islanders recognized that we were of good character. I felt welcomed and comfortable, almost the way I felt living in Harlem. I got to know my neighbors and they would watch out for the children while I worked. We greeted each other warmly and respected each other's space and privacy. I became intrigued by the politics and felt very close to the running of the Island. For the first time in my life, I could identify with the political leaders. They were, for the most part, Black and in some instances my neighbors. It was fascinating to live in a place where I knew the politicians on a first name basis, and walked and talked with them without being discouraged. Moreover, the children had role models that looked like them that they could relate and identify with, and who were available to them. I never had that experience living in New York because most of the politicians there were white and removed from my community.

Even though I was accepted by my neighbors and co-workers, I found it difficult to develop close friendships. Although most of the people were nice to me, they maintained a certain distance. I thought that it was because I was not from the Island. Moreover, I was from New York City and many people are suspicious of Black New Yorkers. Many have the impression of Black New Yorkers as being unsavory characters who are not to be trusted. That image is promoted by the media and generally accepted by those who do not know any better. So, although people were polite, they did not totally accept me into their lives and I did not try to press the issue. Most of the friends I had were Ellis' friends, which limited the kinds of things I could do and say with them. I missed the close friendships that I left behind in New York. Although Rosetta and I spoke on the telephone frequently, I missed going places and spending time with her. I missed our family gatherings where we danced, laughed, ate, and had lots of fun. Although the people I befriended on St. Croix were friendly and nice, I missed the closeness of my childhood friends. The homesick feelings would come and go and as time passed, the episodes of feeling homesick diminished. The more time I spent with myself, getting to know, understand and love myself, the less I missed my friends.

Whenever Ellis was on the Island, we would go out to different places. We both loved to dance, so we would go to various night clubs to eat and dance. When we did not feel up to going out, we would stay home with the kids and play games, play music and dance. Life was quite enjoyable. Everything seemed agreeable, even going to work, because the work environment was not stressful. The children did not have fights in school nor while playing with their friends outside. I did not have to be concerned about the possibility of Karen being molested or Kamal being abducted. Those were constant fears that I had while living in New York. The longer I lived in St.Croix, the happier I became. I did not have to fight anymore. I began to trust people more and realized that many of the situations I found myself in, when I lived in New York, were as a result of my own mistrust and ambivalence towards people.

For the first time in my life, I felt truly happy. It was not because of Ellis or anyone else, it was because I was happy with myself. During my years on St. Croix, I learned how to spend time alone and to enjoy my own company. The stress, clamor, hustle and bustle of the big city was gone and I had the opportunity to relax. A type of peace came over me that I never knew existed. I felt as though I was finally living and not just existing. Life was exciting and full of joy. As a result, I viewed the world from an optimistic perspective. Of course, everything was not always going as smoothly as I would have liked, but I learned how to cope with those types of situations. I learned how to be calm, take quiet time to think and trust that everything would work out fine. I learned to trust and be guided by a higher power than myself. By taking quiet time, I learned how to hear and feel God's spirit. In time, I learned how to be obedient to God's directions for my life. My outlook on life had changed. My understanding of God's will helped me accept the many difficult times that I experience and the many difficult decisions that I had to make. For instance, that positive outlook helped me cope with Karen's departure to attend college in Virginia. For the first time in her life, she was going to live away from me. I had become accustomed to taking care of her, loving and guiding her, and then the time came for her to leave. My heart ached because I wanted my baby back, but no more would she need me in the same way. It was time to let her go find her way in the world. My precious gift from God was ready to spread her wings and fly away, only to return for short visits. Although it was hard for me to accept initially, I did accept and adjust to her leaving through my new found faith. I discovered that I was never alone, that a force of love was always present within me and all I had to do was be still and I could feel the love. So when Karen left, I stood still and felt the overwhelming love that assured me that everything was going to be all right.

The longer I stayed on St.Croix, the more in tune I

became with myself. Most evenings, I would sit on my porch and feel the presence of my inner spirit. In the stillness of the night, instead of crying for somebody to love me the way I did in the past, I was able to hear a voice from within, that I had never listened to in the past. The voice warned me against relying on others to make me happy, but instead, helped me feel the love that lived within me. Sometimes the feeling of love within me was overwhelming. I would silently sob and, with outstretched arms lift my face to the sky. A warm soothing feeling would come over me. A feeling of complete and unconditional love. No longer did I feel I needed to seek love and approval from others. For the first time in my life, I recognized myself as an important and valid individual. I no longer needed to seek attention and approval from my mother, a man or anyone else to validate my existence. How wonderful it was to finally realize that I mattered and had the right to be myself. I was a wonderful, loving person who deserved to be happy regardless of what anyone else thought. Moreover, I deserved to be loved without compromising my values and standards.

The longer Ellis and I continued to see each other, the more distant we became. He did not like my new way of thinking because I no longer depended on him for everything, including my self-esteem. Our relationship had been built on my dependency on him. It made him feel needed and important while it demeaned my self-worth. I was growing stronger and more confident and he was feeling less important. He needed to be in control and I no longer needed to be controlled. Although he remained an important father figure to Kamal, he could not and would not accept me as a self-confident, self-reliant woman. Our relationship was changing for the worse and it became questionable whether it would last. He started staying away for longer periods of time and when he did come to St.Croix, he would always have other things to do. When he came home late most evenings, Kamal and I would have already eaten, so we no longer shared that special family time that we had come to enjoy over the years. Things were falling apart and although I wanted us to stay together, it could not be under the terms of my dependency on him. So, as much as I wanted us to stay together, it was inevitable that it would end. We both had grown to love each other, but I no longer was the same dependent, self-pitying person that he met on the patio in St. Thomas four years earlier. When I tried to talk with him about us, he refused to address the issues and would say that he didn't want to hear about any spiritual growth nonsense. We were not connecting on a spiritual level, so we were destined to part. I understood that for two people to be truly happy together, it must be God's will and when it's God's will then the spiritual connection will be there.

Life looked different for me now. After four years of being together, when Ellis and I began to experience problems in our relationship, I no longer internalized it, as I had been conditioned to do in the past. I did not blame myself when I saw him with another woman at a supper club after leaving my bed and telling me he was going to a political meeting. My inner voice had directed me unwittingly, to the place he had gone. I was not looking for him and had no intentions of discovering him there. I just wanted to go out and found myself at that place. I did not blame myself when, he drove by me as I tried to flag him down, after he and the woman got into his car and drove off. Although I was hurt and cried for the love we lost, I did not blame myself when he came home and I told him to leave. No longer would I behave like a victim. Instead, I decided to accept the circumstances of my decisions and acted accordingly. I decided to accept responsibility for my past actions. He was a married man with whom I carried on a love affair. I should not have been surprised that he would go out with someone else. Evidently, he needed to feel needed and in control and I no longer could satisfy that need. No one forced me to do the things I did. I made my decisions and would stand by them, finally knowing that in my heart I was doing what was best for me.

As he reluctantly started packing his belongings, I thought about some of the disappointments in my life; parents who could not express their love to me verbally, a family who gave me limited encouragement and had been critical and demeaning, my not pursuing the career of my dreams, a broken marriage and my children being raised without the benefit of experiencing their fathers' love. Those things no longer impacted me the way they had in the past. I no longer felt devastated and victimized. The realization that parents are people and people are not perfect helped me to forgive my parents and all of the people who had inadvertently hurt me. I accepted and understood my siblings' feelings toward me and realized that I should be supportive of them, regardless of the manner in which they treated me in the past. I realized that my outspokenness, coupled with my adventurous spirit evoked feelings of inadequacy and jealousy in them. These feelings caused them to act out in a hostile manner toward me. It was a liberating feeling to forgive and let go of past disappointments. I realized that no one was responsible for my feeling good about myself, that was solely my responsibility. The time had come for me to accept the responsibility for making myself happy.

I reflected on my relationship with my father, who I never got a chance to really talk to extensively. I finally realized that there always existed a void in me because I never really knew who he was, how he thought, or what his joys and sorrows were. After his death, sometimes in the stillness of the night, I would sometimes feel his presence, and in dreams I would see his knowing smiles, but he never said anything and I could only guess what he was thinking. As I thought about him, I realized that I sought out older men to express and recapture the love I felt for my father. My thinking was that somehow their expressions of love toward me would substitute for the unspoken love my father had for me. It no longer seemed important to me that my father never verbally told me he loved me. My spirit reassured me that he always loved me and his spirit would continue to love me. So what if it wasn't said verbally. My heart knew. I thought about all of those years I wasted wallowing in self-pity because I wanted to hear my father say he loved me. He was who he was and I had no right to try to impose my will on him.

I also thought about my mother, whom I also held as a

mental hostage because she never told me she loved me. Again, I realized that it was not necessary to be said. When I thought about all of the loving things my mother did for me and my siblings, my heart ached. I remembered the loving meals she prepared each day, the way she struggled to make ends meet, the humiliation she endured from disrespectful social workers just to ensure that we had a clean home to live in, and the way she vehemently and aggressively sought police protection for Richie when his life was being threatened by the gangs. There are no words to express that kind of love. I realized all of the love that I had for Ma and knew, in my heart, that she understood and loved me too.

As I continued to think about love, my heart felt Rosetta's protective love. Her wise and knowing love for me. I thought about how even as a young child, she taught me that I had to exercise some self-control and not say the things that other kids said just because it was the thing to say. I was then able to forgive her for telling on me when I used the word "pussy," when we were younger. In my heart, I realized that her telling on me was an act of love. I thought about all of the wonderful times that we spent together as children and adults and the fact that we always had each other's backs. When I thought about those wonderful times, I realized how blessed I was to have a wonderful friend like her in my life.

As I continued to reflect on my life, I thought about the many unwise decisions I had made. I thought about Shelton and the fact that I made the decision to marry him even though, in my heart, I knew neither of us was ready. Had I been attuned and obedient to that soft knowing voice (my spirit) inside of me, I would not have gotten married when I did. Neither would I have gotten together with him years later, planning to have another child, especially since he was not a good father to Karen. I finally understood and recognized my shortcomings. I realized that it was not Shelton's fault that I was not strong enough or in tune with myself to say no. I no longer was angry at him, instead I accepted my responsibilities in that relationship and was able to forgive myself. It was in the past. It was finally over in my heart and mind. I finally felt free and clear headed. It was as though blinders were removed from my eyes. I could see clearly and I began to smile.

I smiled because I also realized that I entered into the relationships with married men out of anger over the loss of my husband to another woman. Subconsciously, by dating married men, I was getting revenge for my failed marriage. I thought about those and other relationships and also realized that because of their marital status and other barriers, they were unavailable. I finally realized that I accepted those relationships because they were safe. I would not have to really commit myself to them because I feared being disappointed and betrayed again. I realized that I had been acting out of fear, fear of being rejected. Throughout my life, even as a young child, I felt rejected. Rejected because I was a girl instead of a boy. Rejected because of the way I looked. Rejected because of my skin color. My dreams and aspirations were rejected by those in authority, who professed to know what I would be better suited to do in life. And as I surrendered my self-esteem to them, I then blamed them for taking my smile away. But, as he continued to pack, I realized that no one took my smile away. I had given up smiling. No one could take my smile without my consent. I further realized that I was sending out negative energy which attracted the same. I stopped smiling because I stopped believing in myself. That's why I constantly found myself in no-win relationships. I was looking for superficial external gratification instead of looking for the love and endless possibilities inside of me.

I finally recognized the power that lives within me. The power to love. The power of positive thinking. I learned to think good thoughts about myself and those around me. Moreover, I realized that I did not have to tolerate negative behavior from anyone. The power to block out all negative thoughts and people was in my control. I decided to take control of my life. I did not need Ellis or anyone else to give me a feeling of fulfilment. What I needed, I already had. The love of myself and recognition that if I made up my mind, I could accomplish anything. That day, I decided not to dwell on the past, but instead focus on the present and plan for the future.

When he finally finished packing, I was able to watch him leave and not feel alone and afraid. Although I had no family or close friends on St.Croix, I realized that I was never alone. That wonderful inner voice was always with me. I knew that was God's everlasting presence. No longer did I need to feel alone and afraid. All I had to do was be quiet and feel the love within me and I knew that I would attract the same type of love from others.

As I became more attuned to my inner self, a sense of calmness and love consumed me. I began to reach out to others with love and not expect anything in return. Although Karen had gone away to college and Kamal was becoming more independent, I trusted that God would take care of them as I devoted my life to helping others. As I went about helping and loving others, God continued to bless me and my family. I learned that I did not need to depend on men for financial support. All I needed to do was be the best that I could be and things worked out. Even today I do not look back and try to figure out how I made it through the many rough times that followed my breakup with Ellis, because I allow God's will in my life. Even when the going got really rough and there seemed to be no remedy in sight, God always provided the ways. I learned how to be humble and give praises and honor to God. By allowing God's everlasting spirit into my life, I became able to withstand the turmoil of life, with grace.

I continued to trust in God's everlasting love when Kamal and I survived the devastation of hurricane Hugo which destroyed our home and left us homeless on an Island where we had no family or close friends. As a New Yorker, I knew nothing about hurricanes and their destructive powers. While we were alone in our home with no family to support and comfort us, Kamal and I weathered the fierce storm. With God's help I was able to be strong for Kamal, who was frightened, but kept asking me how I felt. The deafening howling winds took part of the roof off of our house (that we had recently moved into), ripped our Mango trees from their roots and tossed them on top of our neighbor's house. We survived the tornados that spun debris around in their cores and then spit them out hurling them with, seemingly, the force of missiles into undeserving targets, but somehow we survived. We lost all of our possessions that were in the house. Kamal handled the ordeal like a little man. He seemed to want to protect me and even today, is protective of me. For three days after the hurricane, we lived in my car. On the fourth day, a co-worker of mine allowed us to stay with her until we could get a flight to New York. During our stint with homeless, my family and friends in New York were extremely worried since they had no way to communicate with us to determine whether we were alive and well. On the seventh day after the hurricane, we caught a flight to New York and I called Ma when we were thirty minutes outside of New York to let her know that we were on our way home. When we got off of the airplane, Ma and Rosetta were waiting for us with open arms and I recognized the love. I also recognized that it was God's will that we return home, to New York, even though I did not want to return. However, God had other plans for me, so I had to obey.

I survived that ordeal and was then faced with starting all over again, trying to find a job, enrolling Kamal in school and deciding what I was going to do and where I was going to live. I still did not want to live in New York, but with no money or job, I had to stay there until I could afford to move elsewhere. I no longer wanted to subject myself to the fast pace of New York. My spirit was no longer happy there. I needed a slower pace and with my faith, I knew that everything was going to be all right. As I began to rebuild my life, an inner strength that allowed me to endure, took hold of me. My life was changed. The things I used to do, I had no desire to do anymore. My outlook on life had changed, and people recognized it. The friends I had before, who were still into partying all of the time, no longer cared to be around me. They seemed uncomfortable being around me, even though I did not talk about my new outlook on life. They could just feel that I had changed. The power of the almighty spirit was with me and I prayed that my friends would also allow his love to abide in them. I began to think of all the wonderful possibilities that life has to offer. No longer would I give in to living life in a pessimistic manner. Life is what we make it. It's about the choices we make. I learned, when I need to make decisions, to pay attention to that quiet voice inside. By being quiet, I am able to get in touch with my inner self, my strength. And although I still make mistakes sometimes, realizing that I am not perfect, I accept the consequences of my mistakes, allow myself time to mourn, forgive, and move on. Life is too short to wallow in sorrow and despair. I learned how to heal by letting go of the past mistakes, disappointments, hurts and pain and instead began to concentrate on living a love filled life. There was no longer time for me to try to control how I thought people should treat or react to me. I finally accepted the right for people to be themselves and choose their own paths and am no longer devastated if I am not included. I stopped trying to live life in a carefully designed, inflexible manner. I decided to let go of the pain and live. Life is short and is meant to be enjoyed. It is a gift from God, to be cherished and used to promote the love that lives within each of us.

My life experiences taught me to take time and enjoy the gifts of the Creator. Things that we take for granted, that are around us but we do not appreciate. I began to feel, with outstretched arms, the wind on my body, realizing that it could not be seen, but knowing that it exists for all of us to feel and enjoy. I learned to look at the sky, the clouds, the sun, the moon, the stars, the darkness and appreciate them all. When once I dreaded the changing seasons, because I was afraid of the unknown, I now appreciate each season for the gifts they bring. The cold Winter snow that cleans the land. The Spring rains that cause the flowers to grow. The Summer sun that warms our souls. The Autumn winds that blow the wilted leaves off the trees and prepare the earth for another cycle of life.

Most of all, I learned to know and love my own heart.

ORDER FORM

Order *Every Heart Knows Its Own Sorrow* as
a gift to a friend or loved one.

Ship To:

Name _____

Address _____

City, State, Zip _____

Phone _____ Fax _____

Quantity	Unit Price	Subtotal
	$14.00	
	Tax (5%)*	
	Total	

* *Tax Subject to change based on Maryland State Tax Laws.*

Please make checks or money orders payable to:
ANSUN ENTERPRISES
P.O. Box 1283
Cockeysville, MD 21030

E-mail Address:
ANSUNENTPRISE@Hotmail.com

For bulk orders please call:

1-800-275-0077

ORDER FORM

Order *Every Heart Knows Its Own Sorrow* as
a gift to a friend or loved one.

Ship To:

Name _____

Address_____

City, State, Zip _____

Phone_____ Fax_____

Quantity	Unit Price	Subtotal
	$14.00	
	Tax (5%)*	
	Total	

* Tax Subject to change based on Maryland State Tax Laws.

Please make checks or money orders payable to:
ANSUN ENTERPRISES
P.O. Box 1283
Cockeysville, MD 21030

E-mail Address:
ANSUNENTPRISE@Hotmail.com

For bulk orders please call:
1-800-275-0077